# AN INTRODUCTION TO
# PRUNING

# AN
# INTRODUCTION TO
# PRUNING

PATRICK JOHNS

GALLERY BOOKS

A QUINTET BOOK

First published in the United States in 1991 by
Gallery Books, an imprint of
W. H. Smith Publishers, Inc.,
112 Madison Avenue, New York, New York 10016

ISBN 0-8317-7199-2

This book was designed and produced by
Quintet Publishing Limited
6 Blundell Street
London N7 9BH

Creative Director: Terry Jeavons
Art Director: Ian Hunt
Designer: James Lawrence
Project Editor: Caroline Beattie
Contributing Editor: Carol Hupping
Illustrator: Rob Shone
Photographer: Patrick Johns

Typeset in Great Britain by
Central Southern Typesetters, Eastbourne
Manufactured in Hong Kong by
Regent Publishing Services Limited
Printed in Hong Kong by
Leefung-Asco Printers Limited

Gallery Books are available for bulk purchase for
sales promotions and premium use. For details
write or telephone the Manager of Special Sales,
W. H. Smith Publishers, Inc., 112 Madison Avenue,
New York, New York, 10016. (212) 532 6600.

*The Author and the Publishers would like to thank the
Royal Horticultural Society, Wisley, for permission to
take photographs in their gardens.*

# CONTENTS

CHAPTER ONE

# THE WHYS AND HOWS OF PRUNING

Although there is a random kind of pruning in Nature, when winds snap off branches or unexpected cold spells harm tender new growth, you cannot rely on this haphazard approach to bring the best results. To prune properly, you have to know the needs and limitations of different plants, and also have a very clear idea of what you are trying to achieve when pruning.

One of the most common reasons for pruning is to keep individual plants (particularly those in small gardens) looking neat and tidy. However, grooming plants can do more harm than good if you inexpertly cut away potential flower or fruit buds and old wood which will not send up new shoots. And indiscriminate hacking to keep a plant within bounds (especially when done at the wrong time of year) can lead to even more vigorous growth and be completely self-defeating.

This book can help you avoid those sorts of frustrations and the common pitfalls that often accompany a home gardener's attempts at pruning. Learning how to prune well pays dividends, since every cut will be an investment in the future of your plants. Good pruning is a matter of understanding why certain cuts have to be made, when they should be carried out, and which are the best tools for the job. Pruning is also a matter of gaining experience, and the sooner you set about tackling those plants that need cutting back, the sooner you will see your garden transformed into a healthier living picture.

Before tackling pruning techniques in detail, we must consider the main objectives involved in modifying a plant's growth pattern so that it flourishes in your particular garden. Not necessarily in order of merit, these are:

to train and maintain shape, maintain health, control growth, stimulate or reduce vigor (as circumstances dictate), conserve plant energy, maximize yield, and rejuvenate the plant (the last two are dealt with in chapter 8).

## TRAINING AND SHAPING

There is no doubt that on young plants any form of pruning will usually delay flowering and fruiting for a year or two. However, this delay is far outweighed by the advantages gained from proper training. With few exceptions pruning should generally complement the natural shape of the plant, so it is important to keep the ultimate form in mind when pruning a young specimen; you should also note that pruning is not a technique for keeping down the size of a large plant. If you do not have the space for what will grow to be a large specimen, do not plant it. Any attempt to limit its size in the mistaken belief that a plant cut well back will remain small more often than not results in quite the opposite effect, especially when the work is carried out during the dormant season.

## MAINTAINING A HEALTHY PLANT

In this area in particular, prevention is always better than cure. Fortunately, the majority of diseases in plants can be avoided with due care and attention, and pruning is a key part of this process. The removal of congested growth in the center of the plant helps to prevent stagnant, moist air from settling there to create conditions favorable to fungal diseases. Not only will air circulation be improved, but sunlight can penetrate to ripen the young growth and strengthen it to help the plant withstand a hard winter. This thinning out of the

**ABOVE** If allowed to go unchecked, plants will most often develop some amount of congested growth in their centers. Prune this out regularly to allow light and air in and to prevent shoots from rubbing against one another.

it easy for spores to infect that area. Whenever possible, and certainly in the case of trees and shrubs, the sideways-growing shoot should be cut away. Shoots partly eaten by grazing animals must also be cut back: they are seldom taken away cleanly to the position where they would be pruned.

Another source of damage is loose, broken branches that tend eventually to strip the bark from otherwise sound wood. These branches are best removed long before they have the opportunity to do further damage. Extra care should be taken when the branch is large, or well above ground, since it can all too easily fall on other, younger branches, badly damaging them.

**LEFT** *Diseased parts are best removed as soon as they are discovered.*

**BELOW** *When two shoots rub together they cause an abrasion, so the offending shoot should be cut out before it has a chance to cause damage.*

center can also lead to more robust growth on the otherwise shaded part. On all plants this will result in a healthier and better-shaped specimen, and on a fruiting plant the crop will ripen evenly on every part of the plant.

### Removing diseased and dead tissue

It is essential to cut away any diseased tissue, to prevent the infection from spreading into the main framework of the plant, or in the case of a tree, into the trunk. Such infection could lead to early death of the plant, or at least major surgery. Removal also prevents the risk of disease spores being carried elsewhere by wind or insects. It is equally important to cut away any dead tissue, since even if it is not already infected, it is liable to harbor disease at some stage.

Whenever diseased or dead tissue is removed, it is important to cut back into healthy tissue beyond the internal staining caused by the infection.

### Abrasions and broken branches

Inevitably, a plant will produce some crossing shoots. Shoots rubbing together cause an abrasion, which makes

It is important to remember that pruning is not a subject in isolation and that, although you can remedy many problems with careful pruning, it is no substitute for proper planting, feeding, and, watering. For example, spindly growth can be caused by a sun-loving plant growing in the shade; insufficient light levels cause pale leaves and weak shoots, making them prone to disease; and lack of nourishment can also cause pallid growth. Unless all these deficiencies are remedied, it is unlikely that a plant will flourish no matter how well you prune.

## Water sprouts
In contrast to weak growth, plants sometimes produce overly vigorous vertical shoots known as water sprouts, particularly from around the area where a branch has been removed. These sprouts may be desirable in plants grown primarily for the color of their stems (when they can be encouraged by hard pruning each year), but for plants grown

## CONTROLLING GROWTH
Some plants have a tendency to produce shoots close together and parallel to each other. This has two adverse effects. First, it robs the plant of light, and second, because each shoot is in strong competition with the other, it leads to weak and spindly growth. Fruit trees such as apple and pear are particularly prone to this problem. Where parallel shoots are growing less than 12in (30cm) apart, remove the one that is of least benefit to the plant.

## Weak shoots
Even the best-grown plants occasionally produce weak shoots. This can be caused by too many buds developing at the same time too close together; if this happens, thin out the congested growth by cutting away some of the shoots so that more light and air can pass through the plant; but avoid removing shoots that will fruit or flower. The best time to prune most plants producing too many shoots is while they are still in leaf. However, certain plants (see the plant lists in Chapters 3–9) should be pruned after leaf fall, since they otherwise tend to lose too much sap.

**ABOVE** *Remove broken and damaged branches as soon as possible, otherwise they are likely to cause a larger wound by stripping bark from the plant.*

**BELOW** *Shoots growing too close and parallel to one another cause shade, resulting in weak growth; give the stronger one more light and air by removing the weaker.*

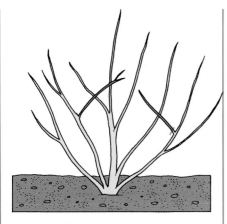

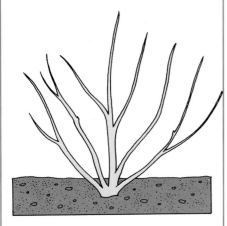

**ABOVE** During maintenance pruning, cut out haphazardly growing shoots. They can make a plant look untidy, shade important growth, and block air circulation.

**ABOVE** *Sappy water sprouts can occur, especially from around the area of the severed branch; they are unproductive and best cut out as soon as you notice them.*

for their flowers or fruit, water sprouts must be removed as soon as they are found. One tell-tale sign is an upright shoot growing faster than others in the framework of the plant.

**Shoots growing towards the center**
Shoots growing in the wrong direction can not only upset the desired shape of a plant – they will also grow toward an open center and can eventually congest it. Such growth must be checked at an early stage.

**Double leaders and multiheads**
Double leaders (main stems) should be avoided in most cases because they are liable to develop into a weak, narrow-angled crotch which will be susceptible to splitting when the branches are abnormally strained, perhaps from the weight of snow. When the tip of a main stem divides in this way, the weaker shoot is best removed. If noticed soon enough, it can be pinched out when the growth is still soft.

**ABOVE** *Avoid double leaders by removing the weaker ones; otherwise a narrow angled crotch susceptible to splitting will result.*

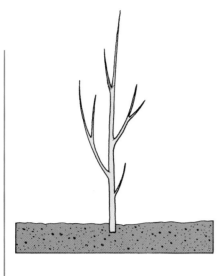

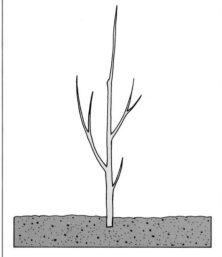

When the tip of the main stem develops two heads it is best to cut off the weaker one – or pinch it off if it is still young and soft.

However, it is natural for some plants, like yew for example, to develop broad multiheads. With these, all leaders should be left on the plant. If your area is susceptible to heavy snowfall, it is advisable to support plants with multi-headed growth by means of strands of wire around the outside, in the form of a girdle. The tie should be placed around the middle of the plant, but not pulled so tightly that the plant is disfigured. As growth proceeds, make additional ties further up the plant and replace existing girdles when they become too tight.

## STIMULATING VIGOR

When two plants, both of the same age and same variety, are planted in different locations, they can produce results that vary dramatically. There are many

**ABOVE** *Some plants, especially certain conifers, produce growing points to form a multihead. Support the growth by tying strands of wire around the waist of the plant (no extra support is needed), but not so tightly that the plant is disfigured.*

**TOP** *When a shoot competes with a leader, it should be removed by cutting back to the main stem.*

reasons for the difference: one plant may be given everything it needs in the way of site, moisture, nourishment, and of course pruning; the other plant may possibly be deficient in one or more of these, and be less vigorous than a plant that has all it needs.

Fortunately, extra vigor within the plant can be encouraged when required by certain pruning techniques. The harder a plant is pruned during its dormant season, the stronger it will grow during the following growing season; lighter pruning will result in comparatively less vigor. This can be seen easily in any woody plant on which one stem has been cut back hard and another has been lightly tip-pruned. The former will have fewer buds to make use of the available nutrients and moisture, and

so subsequent growth of the shoots developing from these buds will be strong, whereas the lightly pruned stem will have more buds to feed, and growth from them will be weaker.

### Notching
Vigor can be stimulated in shoot buds to a certain extent by a process known as notching, which is carried out during spring. Using a sharp knife, remove a small wedge of bark from just above the selected buds. These buds will then be induced to produce shoots when they may otherwise have remained dormant (see Chapter 8).

### Side-shoot pruning
Reducing the number of side shoots on a plant during its growing season will have the effect of making the remaining shoots more vigorous, since the root system will be the same and yet have fewer shoots to support. Such side-shoot pruning is often carried out on herbaceous perennials like chrysanthemums to promote larger flowers.

**ABOVE** *Growth buds can be notched so that when they grow they will be more vigorous. A small wedge of bark is taken away from just above the bud with a sharp knife. The best time to notch is during spring.*

**BELOW** *Disbudding is important for large blooms but must be done with care.*

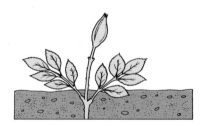

**ABOVE** To get a large single bloom, remove extra buds growing around the central flower bud.

### Disbudding
Disbudding eliminates competition between developing flowers. Carefully remove unwanted buds from around the main flower bud. The flower that is left will be much larger.

11

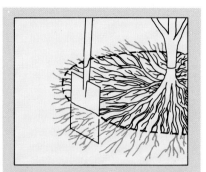

Root pruning a young plant is relatively simple. Push a spade into the soil all around the plant to form a circle with a radius of half the height of the plant, severing roots outside that circle.

## Root pruning

This is an effective way to make a barren fruit tree produce a crop, reduce the vigor of ornamental plants, and encourage root development in young plants. It is best carried out in winter, whenever weather conditions permit.

For young plants, simply insert a sharp spade into the soil at a distance of half the height of the plant all around it so that the ends of the roots are severed. Fibrous lateral roots will subsequently grow.

With mature plants, root pruning is usually carried out to reduce vigor. In the case of a tree or large shrub, first expose the roots by digging a trench wide enough to facilitate cutting the necessary roots, and about 20in (50cm) deep, 2–4ft (60cm–1.2m) from the main stem. It is prudent to treat only half the root zone in any one year and the other half the following year. Any thin, fibrous roots that are not cut by the spade as you dig should not be severed but should be left with as little damage as possible; roots thicker than 1in (2.5cm) should be cut through with pruners or a pruning saw. Remember that one of the functions of the root system is to provide anchorage, so if you cut the roots too close to the trunk or main stem, the plant is much more likely to topple over in a windy storm. Cut the roots not less than half the canopy's width away from the trunk. Tap roots growing downward should also be severed. Once the tap roots have

### ROOT PRUNING AN ESTABLISHED TREE
Only one-half of the roots are pruned at a time; prune the rest the following year.

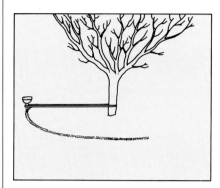

**1** Carve half a circle around the tree at a radius of 2–4ft (60cm–1.2m). Tie a piece of twine the length of the desired radius to the trunk and tie a sharp implement to its other end. Use this implement to mark the half circle in the soil.

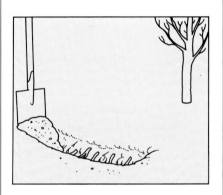

**2** Dig a trench 20in (50cm) deep along the half-circle line.

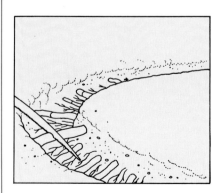

**3** Cut through roots thicker than 1in (2.5cm) with a pruning saw.

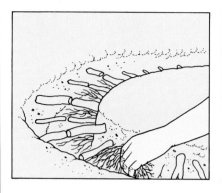

**4** Do not cut through the thin, fibrous roots, but spread them out carefully in the trench.

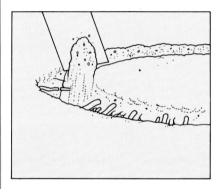

**5** Refill the trench halfway with soil and tamp down on it firmly.

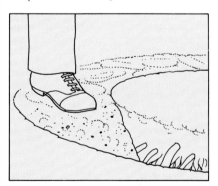

**6** Then fill to the top of the trench and tamp down again.

**RIGHT** *When summer pruning is carried out too soon side shoots grow during the following weeks, and these shoots then need to be pruned. Wait until the base of the shoot is firm and mature before attempting summer pruning.*

been cut, the fibrous roots should be spaced out and the soil can then be replaced, with each layer being tamped down firmly.

## REDUCING VIGOR

Those plants growing on heavy soils containing mostly silt and clay tend to be too vigorous. Such soils retain moisture and plant foods more readily, which encourages the development of strong tap roots in periods of drought. At such times tap roots can reach levels of moisture not available to plants with a shallow, fibrous root system. Generally, excess vigor in plants is produced at the expense of flowers and fruit, so if these are particularly wanted it is in the interest of the gardener to reduce excessively strong growth.

### Late summer pruning

Pruning during the late summer affects the growth rate of the plant and is a useful way of reducing vigor when necessary. Summer pruning also encourages the formation of flower buds and is often used on apples and other fruit-bearing plants.

The right time for summer pruning varies according to the type of plant and should be determined before any shoot is cut. When carried out too early in the season, before the base of each stem has had a chance to mature, more shoots may develop from the cut stem, counteracting the objective of the pruning. Care should also be taken to avoid cutting away the shoots of ornamental plants that haven't bloomed yet. Remember, too, to check in the list at the end of the relevant chapter that the plant is not one that bleeds when pruned during the growing season.

### BARK RINGING—METHOD 1

**1** Insert the point of a sharp knife into the bark and run it around the trunk.
**2** Cut a parallel ring ⅜in (1cm) lower than the first.
**3** Then remove the strip of bark between the two rings.
**4** Cover the wound with tape, making sure that the tape is thicker than the wound so that it does not actually touch the exposed wood, only the surrounding outer bark.

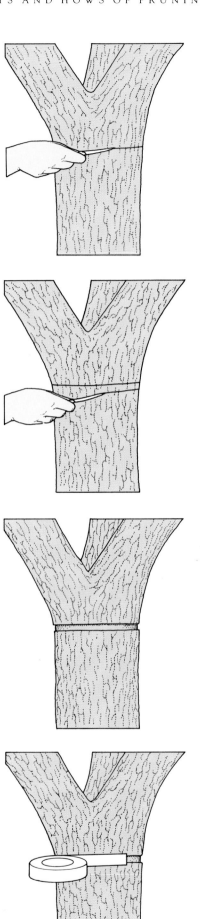

## Bark ringing

Bark ringing should be looked upon as a last resort to control the growth of an over-vigorous tree, because it could seriously damage the plant if carried out incorrectly. However, if it is done with great care, there will be no lasting detrimental effects. The most favorable time to do the job is early summer, when bark can be removed easily.

There are two methods of bark ringing. The first consists of removing a complete circle of bark from around the tree trunk or a branch. To do this, first insert the point of a sharp knife into the bark so that it makes contact with the firm wood below, then run the knife around the trunk or branch until it meets the point where it was first inserted. Cut a similar ring ⅜in (1cm) away from the first and parallel to it, then remove the resultant band of bark. The wound should be entirely covered with adhesive tape (sticking plaster is probably the best) so that it overlaps the edges of the cut without touching the exposed wood. This prevents the wound from drying out so that rapid healing can take place.

### BARK RINGING—METHOD 2

Proceed as in method 1, cutting two semi-circle bands of bark from the trunk rather than one complete circular band. Cover the wounds with tape.

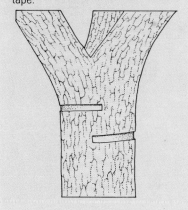

The second method of bark ringing, and the one that is generally recommended since it is less drastic, consists of removing two semicircles of bark. Make a pair of parallel cuts in the same way as for the first method but only to just over halfway around the trunk or branch. Then make two more cuts on the opposite side of the trunk or branch, 6in (15cm) above or below the first, and overlapping them by 1in (2.5cm). Remove the two semicircles of bark and cover the wounds with tape as in the first method.

### Slowing individual shoot growth

Sometimes it is necessary to slow the growth of an individual shoot – for example, one that is growing too vigorously in the wrong direction or one that is already an overly strong grower. Buds at the end of a pruned shoot often produce vigorous shoots, those at the top of the main stem particularly so. The growth of these individual shoots can be modified when they are still in the bud stage by nicking the stem with a sharp knife just below the bud, taking care to avoid damaging the bud itself.

### CONSERVING PLANT ENERGY

In some cases, pruning is done to conserve a plant's energy. An example is removing unwanted suckers, shoots that are produced from the root system, or the lower part of the stem, at or just below soil level. Plants that are grafted

**BELOW** *Individual shoots can be retarded when necessary by nicking the bud before it develops. You can do this by making a cut into the stem just below the bud with a sharp knife, but take care not to damage the bud itself. (Compare this with notching on page 10.)*

**ABOVE** *Remove unwanted suckers arising from below or at soil level, otherwise they will compete with the remainder of the plant.*

onto special vigorous rootstocks (because they do not grow satisfactorily on their own roots) are especially prone to producing suckers. These not only detract from the appearance of the plant but will invariably smother it, and they should therefore be removed the moment they appear. It is important, whenever possible, to remove suckers from the point where they grow from the parent plant. Tear them away rather than cut them off, to make sure you remove all the buds; if even one bud is left, it will grow and produce yet more suckers. Replace any soil you have removed.

### Dead-heading

Much energy is used by a plant in producing a large quantity of seeds, and in many cases the following year's flower display is diminished as a result. The plant produces flower-inhibiting hor-

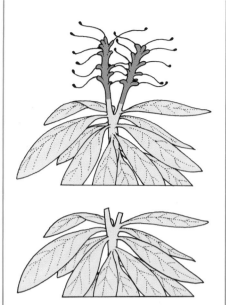

**ABOVE** Remove spent flower heads before unwanted seed heads have a chance to drain energy from the plant.

mones after seed heads have formed, thus ensuring that fewer seeds will be produced the following year and thereby giving the current year's crop less competition and a better chance to thrive. Dead-heading (removing spent flowers) will prolong the flowering period of bedding plants, even encouraging many to bloom throughout the summer months and well into the fall. Dead-heading roses, too, will encourage a second crop of flowers. It is important to remove the spent flowers before the seed heads develop. Dead-heading can be carried out with pruners or, if the flowers can be snapped away cleanly, by hand.

**BELOW** *Suckers are best removed at the point from which they grow by clearing away the soil and pulling off the sucker rather than cutting it away, which invariably causes more shoots to grow.*

CHAPTER TWO

# MAKING THE CUT: TECHNIQUES AND TOOLS

**E**very effort should be made to help a plant recover from its pruning wound. Make sure the cut is as small and clean as possible, avoid unnecessary cuts, and where possible make one cut instead of two.

## THE RIGHT WAY TO PRUNE STEMS

It is important to sever the stem just above a growth bud. This applies to laterals on fruit and ornamental trees, for example, and branches on shrubs and rose bushes. This will usually be more pointed and slimmer than a flower bud, although this rule does not apply to all plants. The reason for cutting back to a growth bud is that extension

**ABOVE** *Buds that develop into blossom are usually fat and rounded, whereas growth buds tend to be smaller and pointed. The round bud on the left of the peach stem will produce blossom.*

**ABOVE** *Make the cut far enough away to avoid damaging the bud, but not so far as to leave a snag. The cut on the far right is correct; the others are not.*

growth will subsequently take place; cutting back to a flower bud would yield just a flower and possibly fruit, after which growth would probably stop.

If you make the pruning cut too close to the bud, there is every chance that the bud will be damaged. If, on the other hand, the cut is too far away, a length of stem is left which is unlikely to heal properly, making it susceptible to disease; a cut sloping in the wrong direction and ragged or crushed stems – the latter are usually the result of blunt

16

pruners – should be avoided for the same reason.

Cut above an outward-facing bud, except on pendulous plants, where the bud should be upward-facing. The cut must be positioned and angled to ensure that the bud is not damaged by the pruning tool and that the wound heals satisfactorily. Cut the stem at an angle, parallel to that at which the bud is growing, making the cut ⅛–¼in (3–6mm) above the bud. The shorter distance is suitable for mild climates when the bud is less likely to dry out; in areas where there is a chance of very low air temperatures, the extra ⅛in (3mm) left above the bud will help to prevent dehydration. Avoid pruning in hard, frosty weather.

## THE RIGHT WAY TO PRUNE LARGE BRANCHES

If lateral shoots are present on an un-wanted branch, remove these first to reduce the weight. Then shorten the branch by stages, leaving a portion about 18in (45cm) long to be dealt with at the end. Make sure that the portions cut away do not damage lower branches as they drop to the ground; large pieces of wood should be lowered gently by rope, which must be in good condition to avoid accidents.

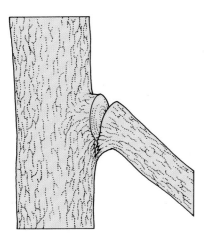

**ABOVE** Avoid ripping the bark of a large branch by careless pruning, otherwise an ugly wound will develop and the plant will be more susceptible to disease.

### THREE STEPS TO REMOVING LARGE BRANCHES

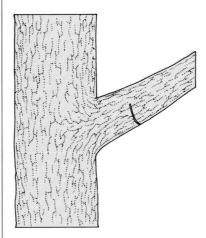

**1** After removing lateral shoots make the first cut 6in (15cm) away from the main trunk, underneath the branch and passing halfway through it.

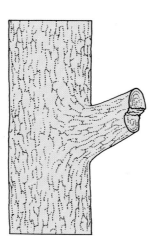

**2** Make the second cut 1in (2.5cm) out from the first and on the top side of the branch.

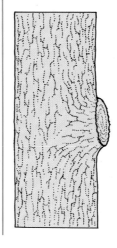

**3** The final cut should be made close to the trunk, just outside the branch bark ridge. It should be angled away from the main trunk so as to form a mirror image of the angle of the ridge. Where a collar is present, the cut should be made just outside it, regardless of the angle.

**4** Then smooth off the ragged edges of the final cut with a sharp pruning knife.

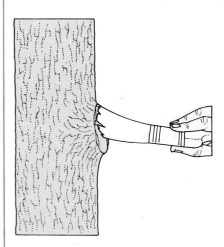

**5** If you wish, cover the pruned area with wound-healing paint (see text).

## Three cuts in all

Before tackling the remaining length of branch, attach a rope to it and secure the other end to a sturdy limb above. Using a saw, make the first cut about 6in (15cm) from the tree trunk on the lower side of the branch and take it about halfway through. Then cut through the branch by making a second cut, 1in (2.5cm) out from the previous cut. This staggered cut will prevent the bark tearing back into retained wood as the branch comes away.

The final cut should now be made just outside the branch bark ridge, angled away from the main stem to form a mirror image of the angle of the ridge. Where a branch collar is present, the cut should be made just outside it, regardless of the angle otherwise the wound is liable to be too large. The final cut should never be flush with the main stem; this would inhibit the tree's natural healing of the wound. Stub cuts (when too much of the branch is left on the tree) should also be avoided for the same reason. Cutting large branches can be tricky. Always aim for a clean, smooth cut. Bark ripped by careless pruning will cause an ugly wound that will be prone to infection.

**TOP** *The branch has been cut away too close for the wound to heal properly.*

**ABOVE** *Stubs are liable to rot when too much of the removed branch is left behind.*

**LEFT** *The branches have been cut off at the right distance from the trunk to ensure quick and neat healing.*

### Smoothing and sealing the cut

In order to keep airborne disease spores from infecting pruning cuts, it is advisable to smooth the surface of saw cuts by using a sharp knife. This will also help to encourage the healing process and prevent rain water from collecting on the surface of the wound and possibly causing rotting.

Wound-healing paint is available to brush onto pruning cuts and, according to one school of thought, will protect the cut from airborne disease spores. However, since there is likely to be a time lapse between pruning and the application of the paint, disease spores may well have time to infect the wound and in that case would be sealed in. Critics of wound painting claim that it is doubtful whether painting has any real beneficial effect, other than to disguise large pruning cuts. It must be said however, that special wound-healing paint has been recommended by some advisers and used with success over the years, although its use has not always been substantiated by recent research work.

## SELECTING THE RIGHT TOOL

There is a vast number of different kinds of pruning implements to choose from. Since they vary in quality and price, it is well worth hunting around for the best equipment in your price range; a well-made tool can last for many years and is a good investment.

Although smaller tools may cost less, it is false economy to purchase one that is not big or strong enough for the job at hand: lightweight tools make hard work of tough stems, and a strained, twisted blade causes damage to the plant as well as to the tool itself. Look closely at the general finish of the product, making sure the handle does not have rough edges and is therefore comfortable to hold with the bare hand – it is not always convenient to wear gloves. Another important factor is the

**TOP RIGHT** *Wounds resulting from branch removal have healed nicely here.*

**RIGHT** *Smooth the surface of wounds using a sharp knife.*

quality of steel from which the tool is made: well-tempered, hard steel (with a bright finish) will keep a sharp edge longer than soft steel, which wears away faster.

How many different kinds of pruning tools you need will depend on the diversity of your plants and the size of your garden. If you need to use large tools only occasionally, it may be hard to justify their purchase. Local tool-rental firms often stock such items as chain saws, which can be rented for a comparatively small charge. However, there is always the possibility that other gardeners may need to borrow a particular tool at the same time that you do,

so if you are unlucky you might end up doing the work later than is ideal.

### Hand pruners

There are basically two types of hand pruners that you can use for stems of up to approximately ¾in (2cm) in diameter. The anvil type consists of a single, straight blade that cuts against a more solid, broader strip of metal (anvil). To use anvil-type pruners, support the stem to be pruned squarely on the anvil, then bring the blade down through the stem. This type of pruner is available in various sizes, to be used on different thicknesses of stem. The blade is easily removed for servicing,

and some models have a notch on the side for cutting wire.

The parrot type of pruner has two curved cutting blades, resembling a parrot's bill in shape, with a scissor action. The design has been modified considerably since it was first produced because the blades sometimes tended not to cut tough wood cleanly. That is unlikely to happen with modern blades, provided you use the tool correctly and do not twist it when you are cutting

**BELOW** *Use a long-arm pruner for the stems that are high up; some types have a curved saw blade attachment to cut off thick stems.*

the stem. This type of pruner is particularly useful for soft stems and for cutting close to a narrow crotch. As with the anvil type, a notch is often provided for cutting wire, and a design with swivel handle grips is also available, which means that if you twist the pruners the blades do not shift.

### Long-handled pruners

If you need to prune stems more than ¾in (2cm) in diameter, it is best to use long-handled pruners, which have strong cutting blades and handles up to 2½ft (75cm) long to give added leverage. They will cut stems up to 1¼in (3.5cm) in diameter and are useful for removing growth from the center of a plant that may be difficult to reach with hand pruners. One type has been designed with self-adjusting jaws, and another with a ratchet mechanism; both make cutting stems of various thicknesses and densities much easier.

### Pole pruners

Pole pruners are useful for reaching high branches. They have a single, usually wooden handle 7–20ft (2–7m) long. The head forms a hooked blade that looks like an inverted J. This is passed over the stem to be cut and then worked by a long length of rope or high-tensile galvanized steel wire. Although you can use pole pruners to cut stems up to 1in (2.5cm) thick, be careful not to prune too large a branch. If the wire becomes strained, it may straighten out at the handle or even break. There is also the possibility that the blade may jam in the stem you are trying to cut. Some models have levers or pulleys that enhance the leverage and allow you to remove large branches more easily.

**TOP** *Long-handled pruners are ideal for awkward areas.*

**RIGHT** *The long-handled pole pruner enables high branches to be cut while standing on the ground, but look out for falling wood.*

### Hand shears

These long-bladed implements are used for clipping hedges and other dense growth, such as some shrubs. They should be used for comparatively soft wood and thin stems – but a notch is usually provided to accommodate obstinate, thicker stems. The blades should be kept sharp by grinding so that they cut cleanly; otherwise too much strain may be placed on them so that they warp and become less effective.

### Curved saws

When access to a plant is restricted, a curved saw often provides the solution. The saw is sturdy, yet comfortable and light to handle. Although the pointed end of the blade is narrow enough to enter a confined space, it can still tackle comparatively large branches. There are short-handled and long-handled versions, the latter allowing you to remove high branches while standing on the ground. This long-armed instrument, known as a pole saw, needs to be used with great care, since high branches can fall with alarming speed after they have been cut.

### Two-edged saws

These saws have a cutting edge on both sides of the blade: one has fine teeth, the other coarse teeth for larger branches. This type of saw needs to be handled carefully to avoid scarring adjacent branches.

### Folding saws

These saws, which can be used only for branches of small diameter, have a blade that folds back into the handle. This is especially useful when you are pruning on a ladder, since when you have finished using the saw it can be slipped into a pocket.

### Chain saws

Chain saws, which are available in various sizes and are powered either by liquid fuel or by electricity, will remove stout branches or fell an entire tree. They are used mainly by professionals, such as foresters and tree surgeons, trained in their use. If you decide to use one, you should take great care in operating it and avoid working from

*When access is restricted, the curved saw provides the answer to many an awkward situation.* **TOP LEFT** *The first cut.* **BOTTOM LEFT** *The second cut.* **ABOVE** *The third cut.*

any precarious position, such as on a ladder. Chain tension is very important and should be checked periodically with the special tool provided with the machine.

**Mechanical hedge trimmers**
Mechanical hedge trimmers are particularly useful for clipping large hedges, saving you time and aching arms. They are also versatile enough to trim shrubs and ground cover. A long blade with sharp teeth moves backward and forward alongside a fixed blade; different models have wide or narrow spaces between the teeth, and it is important to choose the correct one for the particular job to be done. The smaller models cope well with stems up to ¼in (6mm) thick; heavier work requires a larger machine. Look for Teflon-coated blades; these make the trimming even easier and faster.

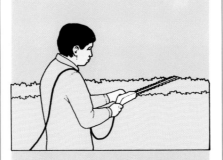

Make sure that the cord of the electric hedge trimmer passes over your shoulder, out of the way of the cutting blades.

Most hedge trimmers are powered by electricity, through an extension cord or from a battery; but gas-powered models are also available. It is absolutely essential that an extension cord be kept out of the way of the blades at all times, whether they are moving or not, since cutting through it could be lethal. It is best to pass the cord over your shoulder so that it is always behind you, not dragging in front of your body. The cord should, of course, be in good condition

and grounded, and be UL-listed. Wear rubber-soled footwear when using a hedge trimmer and use it only on a dry day. Never use the trimmer if you have to stand in a wet spot. Although gas-powered trimmers tend to be heavier, they have the advantage of being safer are able to be used in wet weather.

## LADDERS

You may sometimes need ladders or steps to reach high branches. Aluminum ladders are rot-proof and easier to carry than the wooden kind; the rungs on both are inclined to work loose in time and should be inspected occasionally and tightened if necessary. Hinges are also prone to wear unless they are oiled.

One final tip: if you intend to prune a tree from a ladder, secure this to the tree with rope. In this way any falling branches that rebound from the ground cannot dislodge the ladder.

## TOOL MAINTENANCE

Since even the best of tools will suffer through neglect, good maintenance is essential. A wipe with an oily rag after use usually removes any stains from the blade and, at the same time, gets rid of most disease spores that may have collected on the trimmer. Persistent stains can be removed by steel wool or emery paper.

**ABOVE** *Use a special sharpener to keep the blade keen – or return the pruners to supplier for maintenance.*

**ABOVE LEFT** *A tooth-setting tool is essential for saws, so that they cut properly.*

**LEFT** *A three-cornered file is used to sharpen saw teeth – the special holder keeps the correct angle and spacing.*

CHAPTER THREE

# SHRUBS

Each shrub goes through an annual cycle of growth, leaf development, budding, flowering, and, in some cases, fruiting. Each stage occurs at more or less the same time each year and is influenced by such factors as day length, temperature, soil moisture and, of course, pruning. It is therefore very important to take each plant's life cycle into account when planning how and when to prune it.

While not all shrubs require pruning every year, most are improved by occasional pruning. For example, *Cornus alba* benefits from having older wood cut away, which encourages bright red young stems to appear.

Old shrubs can often be rejuvenated by careful pruning so that they become attractive and productive once more. Very old, congested shrubs can be dealt with most conveniently in two stages: remove dead and weak growth one year, as the first stage of renovation, and carry out the normal pruning recommended for the shrub the following year, as the second stage.

## WHEN TO PRUNE

The initial training of young shrubs should be aimed at establishing a good framework. On young evergreens select three or four strong shoots and remove their tips, cutting back to an outward-facing bud; remove all other stems entirely, cutting them back to soil level. Prune subsequent growth in late spring the following year by thinning out overcrowded shoots. This encourages an open-centered plant through which air can circulate.

On young deciduous shrubs, select up to five vigorous stems and shorten any lateral shoots to approximately half their length, again cutting back to an outward-facing bud. Remove the remaining stems completely. Cut back subsequent growth by half during the following winter and thin out any overcrowded growth at the center.

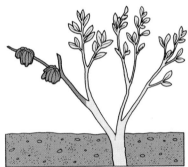

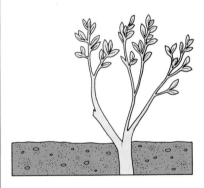

**ABOVE** Shrubs that flower on the previous year's growth should be pruned back hard to new growth right after flowering, in the spring or summer.

**ABOVE** *Cut the flowered shoots of* Erica *back by no more than one-half when the flowers have faded.*

Established shrubs need to be pruned at different times and by different methods, according to whether they are grown principally for their flowers (and/or fruit) or their foliage or stems, and whether, on flowering shrubs, flowers are produced on old or new growth. Detailed information on pruning popular shrubs is given in the alphabetical list at the end of the chapter.

### Flowering shrubs

Shrubs producing flowers on the previous year's growth usually flower during spring and early summer. They include *Forsythia, Kerria japonica, Philadelphus, Pieris,* and *Weigela.* Shrubs like these should have their flowering shoots pruned immediately after flowering so that the plants put all their energy into producing new extension growth rather than developing old wood and seed heads.

Certain shrubs, such as *Hibiscus* and some species of *Berberis,* produce flowers on the current season's growth. Plants

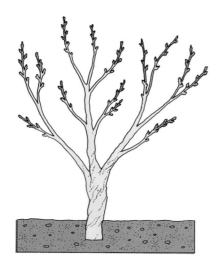

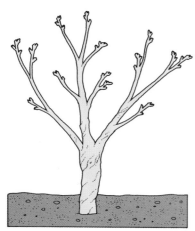

**ABOVE** Shrubs that flower on this year's growth should have last year's wood cut back to two or three buds from the main stem in late winter or early spring, before new growth appears.

in this group often respond best to hard pruning of the previous year's shoots in late winter or early spring, before new growth appears. Some shrubs of this type, such as *Buddleia davidii*, can be very strong growers and, unless pruned in late fall or early winter, may suffer damage from strong winds. (See the listing at the end of this chapter for specific recommendations.)

**Shrubs grown for foliage or stems**
Most shrubs grown for their foliage require only occasional pruning to keep them within bounds. The best time to do this is before new growth starts in spring, since any winter-damaged stems can be removed at the same time.

However, shrubs with brightly colored or interestingly shaped leaves can have these features enhanced by pruning back hard in late winter or early spring. This encourages strong, vigorous growth and large leaves.

Shrubs with variegated or otherwise attractive leaves occasionally produce a single shoot with plain green leaves which tends to be more vigorous than the normal growth. You should deal with such mutations as soon as you notice them, by cutting off the shoots where they arise – otherwise, the entire plant will eventually revert to plain green.

Some shrubs are grown mainly for their brightly colored bark. One of the finest, *Cornus alba,* can be made more striking by cutting its stems back to just above ground level each spring. Others should be pruned less severely. In all cases the new growth produced the following summer is vigorous and matures well to withstand the coldest of winters.

**BELOW** *Brown leaf tips on* Prunus laurocerasus *are winter-damaged. Prune off in spring.*

**BOTTOM** *Cut out mutations such as this on* Weigela florida variegata *as soon as they appear, otherwise you may end up with a different plant!*

# POPULAR SHRUBS

In this alphabetical listing you will find plants organized by their Latin names (with the most popular common names, if there are any, following in parentheses). This is done to avoid confusion, since common names can vary from one area to another. When all the shrubs in a genus are pruned alike, the entry will be listed under the genus name. When specific species have specific pruning requirements, these will be listed separately under their species names.

To help you time the pruning of your shrubs, references have been made to various seasons, like midspring, late winter, late summer, and early fall. These are approximate guides since seasons can vary from year to year and according to which part of the country you live in. But even though they are approximate, they are still useful to follow; any minor delays or deviations from the pruning times given will not be critical.

**Abelia** Prune in mid spring by removing dead and damaged wood back to a healthy bud. Remove stems to keep the plant within bounds.

**Abeliophyllum** (Korean abelialeaf) Once the flowers have faded, cut flowering shoots back hard.

**Abutilon** (Chinese lantern, flowering maple) Prune in late spring by removing frost-damaged shoots and cutting others back to a strong lateral.

**Acacia** Any winter-damaged or overcrowded wood should be cut out in spring.

**Acer** (Maple) Remove shoot tips damaged by frost or wind as soon as possible to prevent necria canker forming on dead wood and then spreading to healthy tissue.

**Adenocarpus** Little pruning is necessary other than dead-heading once the flowers have faded.

**TOP LEFT** Abeliophyllum distichum *is pruned after flowering in spring.*

**LEFT** Acer *stem tips are prone to damage by frost or wind, and should be removed as soon as possible.*

**Aesculus parviflora** (Bottlebrush buckeye) Pruning may be necessary to control the plant's invasive tendencies: cut back branches during late winter or early spring.

**Ailanthus** (Tree of heaven) Normally grown as vigorous trees, the plants can make very effective shrubs when cut back close to the ground in late spring.

**Alnus rugosa** (Alder) Once the catkins have fallen, weak growth should be cut out together with approximately one-third of mature wood. Slow growers should be cut back to encourage a bushy habit.

**Amelanchier** (Serviceberry, shad bush) Old woody suckers should be thinned out in late winter to allow new growth to develop and produce flowers.

**Amorpha** In spring shoots damaged by severe winter weather should be removed and other shoots cut back to the main framework. Old, spent wood is best cut to soil level to encourage new shoots from the base.

**Aralia** The massive leaves should be given room to develop properly by thinning out sucker growths each spring. This treatment will also help to ripen the remaining stems so that they will withstand winter conditions.

**Arbutus** (Margarita, strawberry tree) Any shoots showing winter damage should be cut away during spring, together with spindly, straggly growth. An overgrown specimen may be cut back hard to bring it within bounds.

**Aronia** Little pruning is necessary except thinning out congested growth in winter. This allows air and light to penetrate, which in turn helps ripen fruit later. Invasive suckers should be removed.

**Artemisia** Grown primarily for their leaves and stems, the plants should be cut back hard each spring. The insignificant flowers may be removed as they appear so that the plant utilizes its energy for leaf development.

**Arundinaria** (Bamboo) Early spring winds tend to bruise the leaves, so any necessary thinning out is best done after the weather settles. Most mature shoots should be cut down to ground level – otherwise the clump becomes untidy in appearance – but enough should be retained to support the young growth.

**Atriplex** To produce a bright foliage display, cut shoots back hard to within three buds from ground level in late spring.

**Aucuba** Frost-damaged growth should be cut back to a healthy bud. Each stem should be dealt with individually; generalized cutting back results in severed leaves that become discolored.

**Azalea** Most deciduous azaleas produce a mass of seeds after flowering, which uses up energy at the expense of extension growth and flower bud formation; so dead-head regularly. Very old plants can be rejuvenated by cutting back some mature wood to a bud, from which a replacement shoot will grow.

**Azara** Prune in late spring by removing winter-damaged shoots, those which have flowered, and any that spoil the shape of the plant.

**Berberis** (Barberry) Any dense growth should be thinned out by cutting away stems that have flowered. Prune evergreens immediately after flowering, and prune deciduous plants in spring or

**ABOVE** *When Buddleia davidii buds begin to break during late winter or early spring, cut back to within two or three buds of the main framework.*

preferably summer, when dead wood is more easily seen.

**Bouvardia** In spring remove any winter-damaged shoots and thin out congested growth to encourage new shoots.

**Buddleia alternifolia** (Fountain butterfly bush) This species flowers on wood made the previous year and so should be pruned immediately after flowering in June by cutting the flowered shoots back to a new lateral growth. Overcrowded branches may be thinned out at the same time.

**B. davidii** (Common butterfly bush, summer lilac) This species flowers in late summer on wood made during the current season. Prune before new growth appears in early spring by cutting back all shoots of young plants to a bud within 18in (45cm) from the ground;

all growth of old specimens should be cut back to two buds from the established framework. Cut stems back by half in late fall or early winter to avoid wind rock.

**B. globosa** (Globe butterfly bush) Prune in the same way as for *B. alternifolia.*

**Buxus** (Boxwood) Trim in late spring.

**Callicarpa** Frost-damaged growth should be removed in spring by cutting back to a healthy bud. In mild regions it will be necessary to thin out overcrowded growth from time to time.

**Callistemon** (Bottlebrush) Immediately after flowering in fall, lightly prune, by removing only shoots that have flowered, to promote sturdy growth. In areas with heavy snowfall this will make the plant less prone to damage. Hard pruning should be avoided because growth is slow, or even nonexistent, from dormant buds.

**Calluna** (Heather, Scotch heather) Trim straggly growth in spring, cutting back the previous year's stems by no more than half, since new shoots do not readily grow from old stems.

**Calycanthus** (Sweet shrub) Straggly growth should be shortened by cutting it back after flowering in early fall. Removal of old, unproductive wood and any necessary thinning may be carried out at the same time.

**Camellia** Usually, little attention is needed other than dead-heading. However, some plants tend to grow rather straggly unless tidied by pruning in spring. On spring-flowering species this should be carried out immediately after flowering.

**Caragana** Pruning is only necessary to keep a plant within bounds and should be done when flowers have faded in early summer. These shrubs will tolerate hard pruning if that is required.

**Caryopteris** (Bluebeard) Flowers are often outstanding following a very cold

**BELOW** *Cut the stems of* Cornus *back almost to ground level in spring for a more striking effect later in the season.*

winter that cuts back much of the foliage. Obtain the same result artificially by hard pruning shoots to within 6in (15cm) of the ground in early spring.

**Cassia** Once the shrub is established, little pruning is necessary, other than removing winter damage, thinning congested growth, and dead-heading; this last is best done by cutting back spent flower shoots to mature wood.

**Catalpa** When these trees are grown as large shrubs, pruning will be necessary to keep them within bounds. Flowered shoots and any damaged wood should be cut back in spring.

**Ceanothus** (Wild lilac, redroot) Spring-flowering evergreen species should have any winter-damaged growth removed in spring. Any pruning necessary to keep the plants within bounds should be carried out immediately after flowering, so that shoots will have time to mature for flowering the following year: prune lightly, cutting back laterals to two or three buds and avoiding cutting into old wood.

The summer-flowering evergreen *C. barkwoodii* and deciduous species, which are also summer flowering, require annual pruning in midspring by cutting back almost to ground level.

**Ceratostigma** These shrubs bear flowers on current season's wood; cut this back close to the ground during early spring and remove old or damaged stems.

**Chaenomeles** (Flowering quince) Crossing and misplaced branches are common and should be cut out during winter, together with any that are congesting the center of the plant.

**Chimonanthus** (Wintersweet) Overcrowded stems should be cut back immediately after flowering.

**Choisya** (Mexican orange) Remove weather-scorched stems following a severe winter.

**Clethra** (Summer sweet, white alder) Congested plants should be thinned out during spring.

**Colletia** Remove shoots damaged during winter and, after flowering in spring, prune the plant to maintain shape.

**Colutea** (Bladder senna) During winter shoots should be cut back close to the main framework, and congested growth should be thinned out.

**Cornus alba** (Red-osier dogwood) This shrub produces bright red new stems when cut back almost to ground level in spring.

**Coronilla** (Crown vetch) Shoots damaged during winter should be cut out and remaining growth reduced by half during spring.

**ABOVE** Elaeagnus pungens 'Maculata' is pruned in spring, but cut out reverted shoots as soon as you see them.

**Corylus** (Hazel) Overcrowded bushes should be thinned out after flowering in late spring and any dead wood should be removed at the same time. C. avellana contorta (Harry Lauder's walking stick) tends to throw up suckers from below or at ground level; these should be removed as soon as they appear.

**Cotinus** (Smoke bush) Remove winter damage and do any necessary thinning out in early spring. In addition, hard pruning at that time will enhance the fall color of purple-leaf forms.

**Cotoneaster** No regular annual pruning is required except to restrict the size of the plant and thin out congested growth. Prostrate forms are inclined to produce upward-growing shoots, which should be removed. The best time to prune is late spring.

**Cytisus** (Broom) Stronger-growing species and hybrids can become untidy, in which case young shoots should be shortened by up to three-quarters of their length after flowering. *Cytisus* does not regenerate from old (brown) wood and so it is essential that only young (green) growth is pruned.

**Daboecia** Once flowering has finished, remove half the previous year's growth.

**Daphne mezereum** (February daphne) To prevent long, mainly nonflowering stems from developing, in early summer remove the tips of stems that have flowered.

**Decaisnea** Remove winter-damaged growth in spring and rejuvenate by cutting out old, spent stems during fall.

**Deutzia** All these shrubs flower prolifically, provided old wood that has already flowered is cut out immediately after flowering.

**Dipelia** A large, late-spring-flowering shrub that soon becomes congested. Cut back old spent stems to new growth after flowering.

**Elaeagnus** Remove winter damage and cut the shrub back to required size in spring. The variegated forms are inclined to grow some shoots with plain green leaves from time to time; these should be removed as soon as they are seen.

**Elsholtzia** After a hard winter, frost-damaged stems should be cut down to ground level in spring to promote new growth that will flower in fall.

**Embothrium** An over-vigorous specimen should be cut back lightly during midsummer after flowering. If the plant tends to produce strong leading shoots, these should be removed at the same time.

**Erica** (Heath, Scotch heather) These shrubs should be trimmed after flowering by cutting back shoots that have flowered by no more than half the previous season's growth.

**Escallonia** Vigorous plants growing on fertile soil can be restrained if necessary by cutting back unwanted growth in spring.

**Eucryphia** Growth is inclined to be damaged by low temperatures and affected shoots should be removed during spring.

**Eugenia** Double leaders should be removed at an early stage to avoid weak crotches. Annual pruning during spring consists of removing shoot tips to contain growth and removing any winter damage.

**Euonymus** (Spindle tree) Prune out congested growth in early spring for deciduous plants and in late spring or summer for evergreens.

**Euphorbia** Once flowers have faded, completely remove shoots that have flowered, together with weak growth.

**Exochorda** (Pearl bush) These shrubs are inclined to become very congested unless pruned immediately after flowering during midsummer. Weak shoots

**ABOVE** *Prune* Erica *plants with long-handled shears.*

and most of the older shoots that have borne flowers should be cut back to young growth.

**Fatsia** Cut back an overgrown plant in spring, shortening stems as necessary.

**Feijoa** Once growth has started in spring, winter damage should be removed and the previous year's shoots cut back to mature wood.

**Forsythia** Most of the stems that have flowered should be cut out immediately after flowering in spring, leaving only strong shoots to produce flowers next year.

**Fremontodendron** (Fremontia flannel bush) Cut out winter damage in spring.

**LEFT** *Shrubs flowering during spring and early summer, such as* Forsythia intermedia, *shown here, produce their blossoms on growth made the previous year.*

**Fuchsia** Old stems should be cut back to a bud about 2in (5cm) above ground level during spring, provided the crown of the plant was set just below soil level at planting time; growth buds will then develop from below ground to produce stems that flower during summer and fall.

**Garrya** (Silk tassel) Damaged shoots, together with congested growth, should be removed during late spring when catkins have faded.

**Genista** (Broom, woodwaxen) These shrubs can look very attractive when not in flower, provided the stems are lightly cut back after flowering. Avoid cutting into old wood, which seldom generates new growth.

**ABOVE** *Remove faded flowers to prolong the flowering period of fuchsias.*

**Halimium** The only pruning necessary is to remove, in summer, shoots that have flowered.

**Hamamelis** (Witch hazel) Some varieties tend to sprawl. To prevent crossing and misplaced branches from rubbing, they should be removed during late spring when flowers have faded.

**Hebe** Some of the old wood should be removed in spring to allow room for new growth, which will arise during the following months. At the same time, remove any withered stems caused by severe winter weather.

**BELOW** *Cut* Fuchsia *stems back to ground level in spring.*

**Hedysarum** The loose, open habit of mature bushes tends to make them look ungainly. Any thinning and cutting back necessary to keep the plant within bounds should be carried out during late spring.

**Hibiscus** (Mallow, rose mallow) In spring remove any winter damage, together with the previous year's growth, cutting this back to within three buds of the main framework.

*ABOVE Hibiscus is pruned in spring by cutting the previous year's growth back to leave three buds on each stem. Winter damage should be removed at the same time.*

**Hydrangea macrophylla** (Bigleaf hydrangea) This produces its best flowers on wood made the previous year, so when working around the plant be careful to avoid damaging the large buds at the apex of stems. Thin out the plant in late spring by removing old wood. Last season's spent flower heads may be removed carefully at the same time. *H. paniculata grandiflora* (Peegee hydrangea) should be cut back hard, close to the

33

**ABOVE** *Thin out Hydrangea macrophylla in late spring by cutting out old spent wood.*

mature framework during late spring to maximize flower production.

**Hypericum** (St. John's wort) These shrubs benefit from reducing their growth by half during late spring, after the risk of severe frost has passed.

**Ilex** (Holly) When grown as free-standing specimens, these shrubs should be pruned during winter by cutting back to a bud or a lateral branch.

**Indigofera** These attractive shrubs are rather susceptible to low winter temperatures; any damaged shoots should be cut out during late spring. Remove congested growth at the same time to encourage new growth from the base of the plant.

**Jasminum nudiflorum** (Winter-flowering jasmine) When grown as a free-standing shrub, dense growth should be cut out after flowering during late spring.

*J. humile revolutum* (Jasmine) Any winter-damaged shoots, together with those that need to be cut out to keep the plant within bounds, should be removed during spring.

**Kalmia** (Mountain laurel) Old plants with much unproductive wood benefit from being cut back hard, encouraging new growth to develop.

**Kerria** Cut back any winter-damaged tips to strong new lateral shoots. In congested plants shoots should be removed down to soil level. Remove any invasive suckers.

**Kolkwitzia** (Beauty bush) The graceful, pendulous stems are enhanced by some thinning out during summer when the flowers have faded. This will encourage new growth, which will bear flowers the following year.

**Lavandula** (Lavender) Clip after flowering to encourage a bushy habit.

**Leptospermum** These are tender shrubs that need a protected site in all but warm climates. Remove shoots that have flowered and if necessary thin out at the same time.

**Lespedeza** In temperate zones these shrubs die down to soil level in winter and produce new growth the following spring. In warm areas, where they will maintain a framework of shoots year round, dead wood should be removed, and congested growth thinned out, in winter. Misshapen plants and old specimens may be rejuvenated by cutting them back to ground level during winter or early spring.

**Leucothoë** These shrubs tend to become straggly if untended. Prevent this by cutting back some of the long stems after flowering in spring. A badly neglected shrub can be cut back hard during early spring as a start to reshaping it, though flowers will be foregone that year.

**Leycesteria** To prune in spring, remove the old wood that has lost its attractive green sheen and retain the fresh stems; also cut out any winter-damaged material.

**Ligustrum** (Privet) If necessary thin out each spring by cutting down a few of the old stems to ground level and shortening the longer stems.

**Lindera** Annual pruning is unnecessary, but old specimens can be rejuvenated by cutting shoots back close to the ground during spring, when new growth will arise from the base.

**Lippia citriodora** Winter damage to this tender shrub should be removed during late spring, at which time the previous year's growth should be cut back to within a few buds of the main framework.

**Lycium** (Matrimony vine, box thorn) These sprawling shrubs tend to be rather ungainly unless cut back occasionally in spring.

**Magnolia** These require little pruning other than dead-heading, which should be done with care to avoid damaging the buds below.

**Mahonia** (Oregon grape, holly grape) Some of these shrubs may develop a loose, spreading habit, in which case they should be cut back after the flowers drop in spring. Prune only part of the plant in any one year to retain the grapelike berries that often follow the flowers.

**Melaleuca** These shrubs require a sunny position, which helps to ripen the wood and make it less susceptible to winter damage and therefore less in need of pruning. The plants are reluctant to regenerate from old wood and so need encouragement to produce a bushy habit by having shoot tips removed each spring.

**Myrica** Congested plants should be thinned out during spring; suckers, which can cause the plant to become invasive, are best removed.

**Myrtus** (Myrtle) The only pruning necessary is trimming to maintain the plant's shape in late summer after flowering.

**Nandina** (Bamboo) Canes should be cut out at ground level when the plant starts to become congested.

**Nerium** Winter protection should be given in cold areas. To produce a compact, attractive plant, cut back old wood to the main framework and spent flower shoots to the previous year's growth in fall after flowering.

**Nyssa sinensis** (Chinese sour gum) Trimming is necessary during spring, to restrict the plant to its allotted space.

**Olea** Little pruning is necessary other than removal of winter damage and shortening lateral shoots to maintain an open center.

**Olearia** (Tree aster, daisy bush) Prune by removing old flowering shoots in spring and trim if necessary to maintain the plant's shape.

**LEFT** Phygelius capensis *flowers on current season's growth and is cut back close to soil level in spring.*

**RIGHT** *Prune cherry laurel in early summer after the flowers fade.*

**BOTTOM RIGHT** *Carefully maintained, a hedge will outlast many other types of screen. This lovely flowering hedge is Rhododendron ponticum.*

**Osmanthus** This evergreen needs to be pruned in early spring and again in summer or fall to keep its shape. Pruning later in spring could jeopardize small, very fragrant flowers.

**Osmaronia cerasiformis** This bears flowers on stems made the previous year; carry out any pruning necessary to keep the plant within bounds immediately after flowering in spring.

**Paeonia (Peony)** The only pruning necessary is dead-heading when the flowers have faded, unless seeds are required.

**Perovskia** These shrubs tend to die back during winter. In spring cut all stems back to within an inch or two of the woody base.

**Philadelphus** (Mock orange) Flowering is enhanced the following year by removing flowering shoots once blossom has faded during late summer and fall; cut them back to vigorous new lateral growth. Thin out the plant at the same time.

**Phlomis** Any winter-damaged stems should be removed during spring. Also, prune after flowering in summer by cutting back untidy growth.

**Phygelius** These shrubs can be very invasive, and shoots should be removed at an early stage. In spring cut back the previous year's shoots to ground level to promote vigorous new growth that will bear the current season's flowers.

**Physocarpus** One-third of the old stems should be removed to the base of the plant each spring. Cut back the remainder to one-year-old wood.

**Pieris** (lily-of-the-valley shrub) The only pruning normally required is dead-heading.

**Piptanthus** Remove dead shoots in spring and trim growth to keep it within bounds after flowering in late summer.

**Potentilla** (Cinquefoil, five-finger) These shrubs benefit from being kept fairly open in the center to encourage young growth. Prune by removing old stems in spring.

**Prunus laurocerasus** (Cherry laurel) This shrub can be grown as an attractive free-standing specimen when pruned to keep it within bounds. Prune when flowering has finished in early summer.

**Punica** (Pomegranate) In spring remove winter damage, together with weak shoots and congested growth; spent flower shoots should be cut back to mature wood at the same time.

**Rhododendron** Although hardy rhododendrons will tolerate hard pruning, the only cutting back usually necessary is simply to maintain shape and keep the plant within bounds. It is, however, important to dead-head to promote extension growth, especially when the plant is growing in poor, sandy soil.

**Ribes** (Currant) After flowering in late spring cut leading shoots back by half and thin out old wood.

**Robinia** (Locust) The only pruning necessary is to tidy up broken shoots after a storm.

**Romneya** The soft stems are frequently cut to the ground by the cold in winter. Cut all growth to within an inch or so of the ground in spring.

**Rosmarinus** (Rosemary) Cut back straggly growth in summer after flowers have faded: reduce the previous year's growth by half to encourage a dense, bushy habit.

**Rubus** (Bramble) Cut back to keep growth within bounds. Do this in fall, except for those grown for their silver bark; on these cut old stems to the ground in spring to encourage fresh silver shoots in winter.

**Salix** (Willow, osier) Those shrubs grown primarily for their colored stems are best cut back to within a few inches of the ground during late spring. New stems will then be produced during the following growing season. Prune those grown for their decorative catkins by thinning out congested growth once the catkins have faded in late spring.

**Sambucus** To obtain more foliage and larger flowers, cut laterals back almost to the previous year's growth in late spring.

**Santolina** Trim each spring to keep them tidy and dense.

**Senecio** These shrubs all tend to become straggly unless trimmed in spring, when any winter-damaged shoots can be removed at the same time.

**Sorbaria** Growth can become invasive unless the suckers are removed. Hard pruning, almost back to old wood, in spring is rewarded by more flowers in summer and fall.

**Spartium junceum** Cutting flowers for the home in late summer may be sufficient pruning; otherwise, the plant should be cut back during spring, taking care to avoid cutting into old wood, which does not easily produce new growth.

**Spiraea** (Bridal wreath) Late-flowering spiraeas should be cut back to within 6in (15cm) from the ground in early spring; early-flowering kinds should be lightly cut back, and thinned out if growth is congested, during late spring after flowering.

**Styrax** Remove congested growth in spring to maintain an open center.

**Syringa** (Lilac) Dead-head to encourage more flowers of better quality the following year. Old plants past their best and flowering poorly can be rejuvenated by removing congested growth and shortening branches by one-third in winter.

**Tamarix** (Tamarisk) To prevent the summer-flowering *T. gallica* (French tamarisk) and *T. pentandra* from growing too tall and to promote bushy growth, cut back the previous year's growth by half in early spring. Prune the spring-flowering *T. tetrandra* after flowers have faded by removing old growth and shortening lank young growth at the same time.

**Thymus** (Thyme) These shrubs tend to become congested. Since they soon rejuvenate from old wood, at least half the previous year's growth may be removed during spring.

**Ulex** (Furze, gorse, whin) Mature specimens tend to become straggly and are best cut back during early summer when flowers have faded.

**Vitex** (Chaste tree) In spring remove winter-damaged shoots and cut laterals back to the main framework.

**Weigela** As soon as flowers fade cut spent wood back to vigorous new lateral shoots to ensure a good floral display the following year.

**Wisteria** After flowering in summer, cut current season's growth back by at least half.

**Zenobia** In late spring remove old, spent wood, dead-head, and cut shoots back to active buds.

**LEFT** *Deciduous plants flowering on current season's wood, such as Spiraea 'Goldflame', often respond best to hard pruning during late winter and early spring.*

CHAPTER FOUR

# VINES, CLIMBERS, AND OTHER WALL PLANTS

T he true climbers fall into three categories: plants with their own natural support, such as aerial roots which act as suction pads on a wall or fence; plants that twine their stems, tendril or other parts around a support; and plants with hooked thorns. Other plants, though not true climbers, tend to grow in such a way as to cover structures and are also included in this chapter.

When acquiring a bare-rooted plant, cut off any damaged roots, remove any weak or damaged shoots, and shorten the remainder by half.

## TRUE AND SOFT STEM CLIMBERS

During their first year true climbers and plants with soft stems require very little pruning; they should be allowed every opportunity to establish themselves. In subsequent years follow the instructions given in the plants list that follows. One important general point to remember is that you should remove shoots growing outward, away from the support; do not prune those growing inward because they are needed to provide and reinforce support for the plant.

## WOODY STEM CLIMBERS

For plants that develop woody stems, formative pruning during the early years is needed to establish a good framework. In the case of woody deciduous climbers, it will ensure that during the dormant period, when only the framework can be seen, the plant will still be attractive. Some plants look very good when trained as fans; follow the pruning methods suggested for tree fruits in Chapter 8 to achieve the shape you want.

### PRUNING NON-SELF-SUPPORTING CLIMBERS

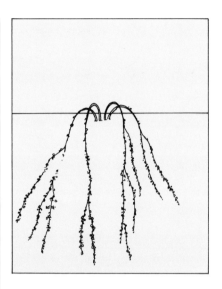

**1** Carefully remove the plant from its support and lay it on the ground.

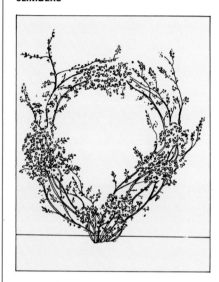

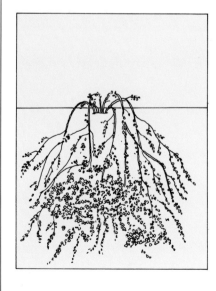

**2** Prune away the dead growth and very old growth with hard bark.

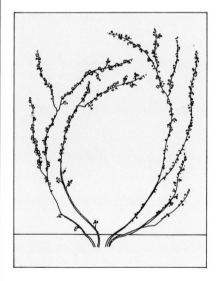

**3** When this is done rearrange the plant over its support and tie it if necessary.

**OPPOSITE PAGE** *Bougainvillea is a vigorous plant and needs space. Cut congested growth back to main framework in autumn.*

# POPULAR VINES, CLIMBERS, AND WALL PLANTS

The following list consists of a selection of true climbers, other shrubs and trees that can be trained to grow up or over a wall or other structure – with or without being tied to supports, and some plants that simply benefit from the protection that a wall gives them. Some of the latter are rather tender, but against a wall they can succeed in areas that would normally be too cold for them.

Those shrubs that can be treated as climbers are listed here, but readers are often referred back to Chapter 3 for the basic pruning techniques for these plants.

**Abelia floribunda** See Abelia in Shrubs. Midspring is the best time to prune by removing dead and damaged wood back to a healthy bud. Reduce stems to keep them within bounds.

**Abutilon** See Shrubs.

**Acacia** See Shrubs.

**Actinidia** Remove dead and spent wood during spring. Since the plant is vigorous, it may need thinning out when growing in fertile soil.

**Adenocarpus** See Shrubs.

**Akebia** Prune during summer after flowering by first removing the spent shoots, then thinning out any congested growth still remaining. Old plants that are not flowering can be rejuvenated by cutting back all top growth to approximately 3ft (1m) from the ground.

**Ampelopsis** Before growth commences in spring reduce the previous year's shoots to within two or three buds of the old wood.

**Aristolochia** (Birthwort) Once the flowers have faded in summer remove congested growth and reduce long shoots by half. Remove winter damage in spring.

**Azara** Shoots that have borne flowers should be cut back to the main framework once the flowers have faded in late spring.

**Bignonia** (Cross vine, trumpet flower) Suckers are best removed at an early stage. Thin out congested growth and weak shoots immediately after flowering, which varies from midsummer to fall according to climate.

**Bougainvillea** Their rampant growth should be given generous space, otherwise they will need to be cut back several times each year. In fall cut congest-

ed growth back to the main framework and side shoots back to two or three leaves. However, if flowering continues until late in the year, this pruning can be delayed to early the following spring before growth starts.

**Buddleia globosa** See Shrubs.

**Callistemon** (Bottlebrush) Remove old spent shoots completely, since the plant is reluctant to break into growth from mature wood. Prune where necessary in the fall after flowering.

**Camellia** See Shrubs.

**Campsis** (Trumpet vine, trumpet creeper) Remove suckers from the base at an early stage. Control growth by cutting back the previous year's growth to two buds in spring. In summer pinch back any untidy shoots to three leaves.

**Carpenteria** Little pruning is necessary other than removing winter damage and congested growth in spring.

**Ceanothus** See Shrubs.

**Celastrus** (Bittersweet) In early spring cut main stems back by about a half to a strong lateral shoot.

**Cestrum** In spring cut back winter-damaged and overcrowded shoots to young side shoots.

**Chaenomeles** (Flowering quince) Prune just before growth starts in early spring. First remove crossing branches and congested growth; then cut back by one-third wood made the previous year. Tear away any shoots arising from the base.

**Chimonanthus** (Wintersweet) See Shrubs.

**Clematis** The only pruning needed by clematis species is the removal of dead wood and cutting back shoot tips to maintain shape. Prune spring-flowering species immediately after flowering, and prune summer- and fall-flowering species in spring.

Hybrids are divided into three groups based on when they flower and on which season's growth the flowers appear. The Florida group flowers in summer, the Patens group in spring, both on the previous year's wood. Both these groups are pruned alike, by cutting back old, spent wood as soon as the flowers fade. If plants become rampant cut them back hard during late winter at the expense of the forthcoming season's flowers. The third group, Jackmanii, flowers in late summer on the current season's shoots. To prune, cut away the

**ABOVE** *Most Hederas are hardy, to withstand cold temperatures, but any winter damage should be removed in spring.*

**BELOW** *Prune spring-flowering clematis as soon as the flowers fade. This is Clematis montana.*

top growth to within 1ft (30cm) of ground level in spring.

**Clethra** See Shrubs.

**Clianthus** (Parrot beak) Cut out weak shoots in late spring and remove spent flower clusters in midsummer.

**Coronilla** See Shrubs.

**Cotoneaster** See Shrubs.

**Cytisus** See Shrubs.

**Daphne mezereum** See Shrubs.

**Desfontainea** Old, congested wood should be removed by cutting back to a strong, well-placed lateral shoot after flowers fade during summer.

**Eriobotrya** In spring remove damaged shoots and those that have flowered.

**Escallonia** See Shrubs.

**Euonymus** See Shrubs.

**Feijoa** See Shrubs.

**Forsythia** See Shrubs.

**Fremontodendron** See Shrubs.

**Garrya** See Shrubs.

**Hedera** (Ivy) In spring remove any winter damage and invasive growth. Variegated forms benefit from thinning and shortening stems to encourage large, well-colored foliage; remove shoots on which leaves have reverted to plain green.

to produce new shoots. Only that part of the plant to be cut away should be removed from its support, since once the stems have lost their attachment, they are unable to regain it at the same point.

**Passiflora** (Passion flower) Winter damage, which may be extensive in some areas, should be cut out, together with weak growth, during spring. Reduce lateral shoots to approximately 6in (15cm) at the same time.

**Periploca** (Silk vine) Prune during early spring, by removing congested growth and weak shoots. The milky latex is said to be poisonous if ingested, so be careful when handling the plant, and wash your hands after doing so.

**LEFT** Hydrangea petiolaris *shoots that are growing outward should be cut back to the main stem in spring, together with old flowered shoots.*

**BELOW** Lonicera *is pruned during spring by cutting out congested growth. Carefully lay the stems on the ground if you can before pruning.*

**Hibiscus** See Shrubs.

**Humulus** (Hops) In spring thin out congested growth and remove winter damage. The plant can be cut back hard to keep it within bounds.

**Hydrangea petiolaris** In spring remove congested growth and cut outward-growing shoots and spent flower stems back to the main stem.

**Hypericum** See Shrubs.

**Itea** (Sweetspire) Little pruning is necessary other than cutting back to maintain shape and size during spring. In a warm climate pruning can be done in fall after flowering.

**Jasminum nudiflorum** See Shrubs.

**Kadsura** The fall tints of these tender climbers can be enhanced by pruning out a quarter of the old growth each spring, to encourage replacement shoots.

**Kerria** See Shrubs.

**Lonicera** (Honeysuckle) Remove congested growth in early spring. In the case of a plant growing through a small tree, if possible detach it and spread it on the ground to make pruning easier.

**Lycium** See Shrubs.

**Magnolia** Branches should be replaced before they become unproductive. Prune evergreens in fall, at the same time tying young growth to its support. Deciduous magnolias are better pruned as soon as flowers fade during summer.

**Myrtus** See Shrubs.

**Olea** See Shrubs.

**Olearia** See Shrubs.

**Parthenocissus** (Woodbine) Rampant growth can be controlled by cutting it back at any time of year. Avoid cutting back into old wood, which is reluctant

rubbed out as soon as possible to avoid an untidy appearance. Otherwise, the only pruning necessary is to cut out some of the shoots that have produced berries, once these have fallen or been taken by birds. Vigorous plants can be pruned in summer by pinching back the soft growth to three or four leaves.

**Raphiolepis** Remove shoots that have outgrown their allotted space once the flowers have faded in late summer; on *R. umbellata*, which produces fruits during late summer and fall, this can be delayed until later in the year.

**Ribes** See Shrubs.

**Rosa** See Roses.

**Rubus** See Shrubs.

**Solanum** (Nightshade) Damaged and weak shoots are best cut back to a strong lateral in spring. On vigorous growers such as *S. crispum* prune previous year's shoots to within 6in (15cm) of the main framework in late spring.

**Tibouchina** (Glory bush) Winter damage should be cut out in late spring when growth buds have become active.

**ABOVE** Pyracantha *shoots growing away from the plant should be removed as soon as they appear. When the berries have gone cut out up to one-quarter of the laterals that have produced berries.*

**RIGHT** *A wall or fence can provide shelter for tender plants, such as this* Solanum crispum.

**Phlomis** See Shrubs.

**Phygelius** See Shrubs.

**Piptanthus** See Shrubs.

**Polygonum** In spring, before growth commences, cut out damaged and dead stems and cut remaining growth back hard to two or three buds, which will produce flowers that summer. After, and possibly during, flowering, it may be necessary to lightly trim back excessive growth. Very old plants can be cut back hard, even to ground level, to regenerate new growth.

**Pueraria** (Kudzu vine) Remove winter-damaged and invasive growth in spring. The plant can be cut back hard if necessary.

**Punica** See Shrubs.

**Pyracantha** (Firethorn) Shoots arising at the front of the shrub should be

Prune spent wood and weak growth back to the main framework in late spring.

**Vitis coignetiae** (Crimson glory vine) When the plant has filled its allotted space, cut the new shoots back to within bounds during late summer. Old wood may be thinned out, preferably in the dormant season, to avoid loss of sap.

**Wisteria** Once flowers have faded in summer reduce the current season's growth to four or five leaves; treat further growth during the year in the same way. The twining stems are inclined to grow beneath shingles and roof tiles: remove them while they are still green, before any damage is done. In winter reduce the shortened stems to two or three buds and thin out congested growth.

**RIGHT** *Wisteria needs pruning just after the flowers fade.*

**BELOW** *Vitis tends to bleed from old wood and so any thinning should be done during winter. Young stems of the current season's growth can be shortened if necessary during late summer.*

CHAPTER FIVE

# ROSES

roses are the most popular of garden plants. Enthusiasts fill every available space with them, but the average gardener will probably be content with a bed of hybrid teas, floribundas, one or two species of roses, or shrub roses in a mixed border and perhaps a rambler or climber trained up a wall, over an archway, or horizontally along a trellis or fence. Miniature roses are attractive and can be grown successfully in containers.

## PRUNING NEWLY PLANTED ROSES

On all newly planted roses, cut back any dead stems to healthy wood, just above a bud. Remove the weaker of any crossing stems, again cutting back to just above a bud. Entirely remove any spindly stems. After this standard

**ABOVE** *Larger blooms result from disbudding.*

pruning, any further initial pruning and subsequent maintenance pruning should be carried out as follows according to the type of rose.

## Hybrid teas, floribundas, grandifloras, polyanthas

In spring, just before growth starts, cut one-year-old roses back hard to buds approximately 4½in (11cm) from the ground. However, if the rose was planted in fall and has very long shoots, these should receive a preliminary pruning after planting by cutting them back by half to avoid wind damage.

Maintenance pruning should also be carried out in spring, before new growth appears. Remove winter damage at the

## PRUNING NEWLY PLANTED ROSES
Newly planted roses are all pruned pretty much the same way, no matter what the type.

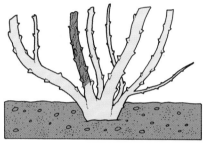

**1** Cut all dead stems back to healthy wood.

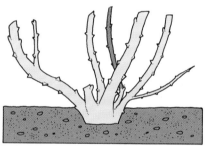

**2** Look for crossing stems and cut back the weaker ones to just above a bud.

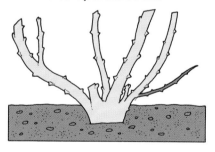

**3** Remove all spindly stems.

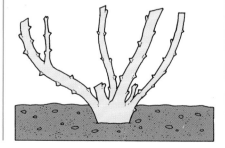

ABOVE *Rose shoots damaged by late frost should be cut back to a healthy lateral.*

same time. The standard spring pruning procedure is first to remove any winter-damaged stems and any dead or diseased wood; next, thin out the center of the bush to allow air and sunlight to penetrate and to facilitate spraying; then cut back any weak growth to one or two buds from the main stem. The extent to which the rest of the plant will need pruning depends on various factors. For example, strong-growing plants require less pruning than weaker ones. However, as a general rule cutting wood made the previous year back by half should provide a good garden display and sufficient flowers for cutting. If you want numerous early flowers it is best to prune more lightly; conversely, late flowering, with fewer, larger blooms and more vigorous growth results from more severe pruning. So you should regulate your pruning according to what you want and what the plant needs.

On weak-growing roses with thin stems, the previous season's growth should be cut back hard, by two-thirds, to produce stronger stems more likely to resist weather damage and to provide better cut blooms.

A second pruning in late fall is beneficial: remove any damaged stems and cut back long shoots to avoid damage from winter winds and cold.

ABOVE CENTER *Light pruning encourages earlier flowering.*

ABOVE *Hard pruning produces sturdy growth and later flowering.*

**PRUNING HYBRID TEA ROSES**

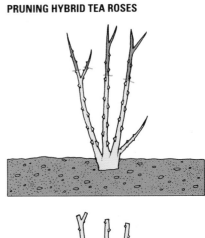

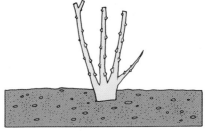

**1** After planting prune away all dead wood and weak and spindly growth.

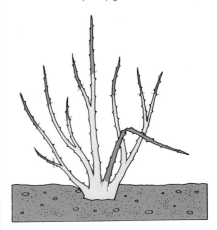

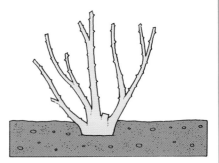

**2** The following spring and every spring thereafter cut back last year's growth by half. Weak-growing bushes can be pruned more severely to encourage growth.

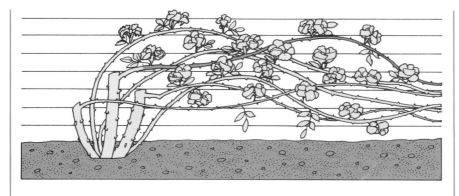

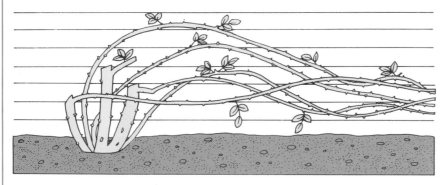

## Climbers and ramblers

One-year-old climbers do not require any initial pruning, other than the standard procedure described. Established plants are best pruned during late fall by cutting back the old flowered shoots to within 3in (7.5cm) of the main stem.

After planting ramblers, cut them back to a bud approximately 1ft (30cm) above ground level – if this has not already been done at the nursery. Prune established plants during fall. You may need to thin out vigorous growers each year by removing old stems to ground level or back to a strong lateral. The only other pruning necessary is to cut back lateral shoots which have flowered to about 3in (7.5cm) from the main stem.

## Climbing sports

Climbing sports can be trained horizontally on frames or wires. With this method, flowering stems develop more uniformly than on an upright plant, since the sap tends to spread through the stems evenly instead of rising to the buds at the tips.

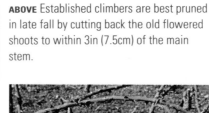

**ABOVE** Established climbers are best pruned in late fall by cutting back the old flowered shoots to within 3in (7.5cm) of the main stem.

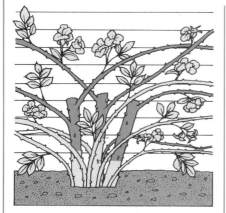

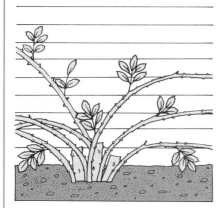

**ABOVE** Established ramblers are pruned during fall when vigorous growers are thinned out by removing very old stems to ground level or back to a strong lateral, where one exists.

After planting, cut back to three or four buds from the union (where the top growth arises from the rootstock). This will encourage vigorous growth the following year. In winter this growth should be tipped back to firm growth and then tied to the framework with garden string. Subsequent pruning consists of cutting old shoots that have flowered back to two buds and removing old congested stems, either completely or back to a strong-growing lateral.

**PRUNING CLIMBING SPORTS**

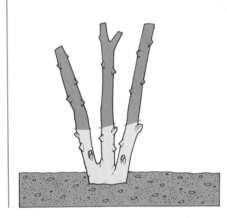

**1** Prune back to three or four buds that emerge from the union at ground level immediately after planting.

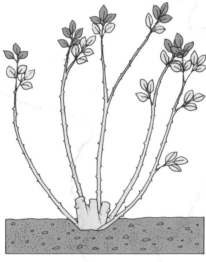

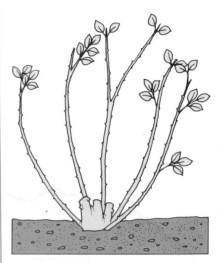

**2** In the winter tip back to firm growth all vigorous growth produced in the previous year.

**3** Subsequently, cut old flowered shoots back to two buds and removing old congested stems completely, or cutting them back to a strong-growing lateral.

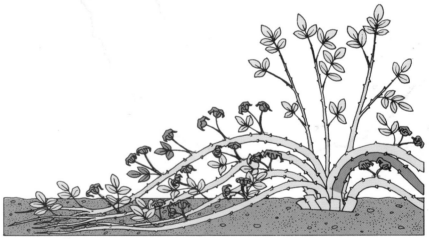

**LEFT** *Climbing sports are trained horizontally on wooden or metal frames, supported just above the ground.*

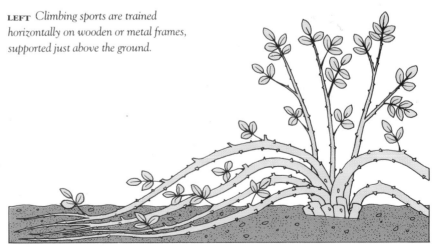

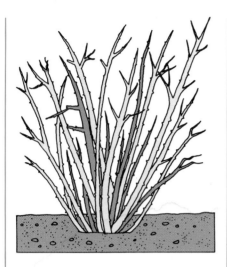

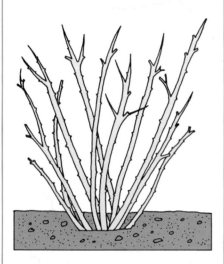

**ABOVE** The only pruning necessary with species roses is to reduce the length of any invasive growth to a strong lateral.

### Shrub roses and species roses

Shrub roses and species roses do not require any but standard pruning immediately after planting. Thereafter, shrub roses need little maintenance pruning other than removing dead or weak growth and thinning out when necessary. For species roses the only pruning necessary is to cut invasive growth back to a strong-growing lateral shoot; anything more drastic can ruin the appearance of the plant.

**RIGHT** *Avoid removing flowers on species roses if possible so that hips develop. Shown here is* Rosa moyesii.

**Miniature roses**
Miniature roses need only have congested growth reduced and dead shoots removed, preferably with scissors.

## CUTTING BLOOMS AND DEAD-HEADING
Cutting blooms during the summer is a form of pruning, since where you cut can ultimately affect the shape of the

**ABOVE** *Miniature roses are effective when grown outside, or indoors on a light window ledge. Pruning is best done with scissors.*

plant. Try to ensure that you cut back the stems to a bud which will grow out in the desired direction. Some roses produce colorful hips that provide an added attraction in late summer and fall. On all other roses faded blooms should be dead-headed to prevent hip production and so help conserve the the plant's energy.

# CHAPTER SIX

# HEDGES

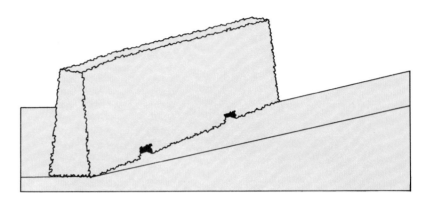

M any gardens benefit from a hedge for one reason or another: it provides privacy, a boundary, shelter from wind, and a screen to hide unwanted views. Hedges are often used to divide features in a large garden, and smaller gardens can be made to look bigger by a well-placed hedge.

## PRUNING NEW HEDGES

Except for conifers, hedge plants generally benefit from light trimming during the first spring after planting: reduce the leading shoots to a uniform height and cut side shoots back to form a straight line. During the following year or two, prune the plants lightly in this way right through the growing season. However, slow-growing plants that are well furnished with side branches need only misplaced shoots removed, while, at the other extreme, fast-growing plants need to be cut back hard to encourage growth from dormant buds near ground level.

On evergreens it is important to complete all pruning by the end of the active growth period, so that stems will have the opportunity to ripen before winter. Otherwise, frost may well damage the soft tissue. With deciduous plants an alternative method is to cut stems made the previous growing season back by half during winter.

## PRUNING ESTABLISHED HEDGES

Once a hedge has reached the desired height, trim it once a year, after the flowers have faded (but bear in mind that with pruning at this time fruit will be forfeited) or, in the case of a non-flowering hedge, in midsummer. More specific guidelines are given in the plant list later in this chapter.

Make sure to prune a hedge so that its base is wider than its top. This will enable the lower leaves to receive a fair share of light. In addition, less damage

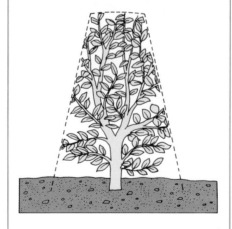

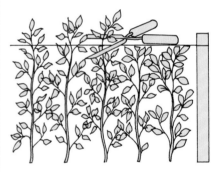

**ABOVE** To protect plants growing higher on a slope from frost in cold regions, cut 6in (15cm) gaps at 6ft (2m) intervals in the base of the hedge growing lower down the slope.

**ABOVE** During their first summer after planting, hedges, with the exception of conifers, will require light trimming by cutting the leading shoots to a uniform height. Secure a taut line between two poles to get this. The side shoots should be cut back to straight lines. Note that the hedge should eventually be wider at the base.

is likely from the weight of snow collecting on the top of a narrower-topped hedge.

Hand pruners are the most convenient tool to use for young plants and informal hedges that are allowed to grow more naturally. They are also the best for broad-leaved plants, since the leaves will not be damaged in the way that they would be by using shears. Mechanical trimmers and shears are ideal for small-leaved formal hedges (those clipped into very well-defined shapes). They should be used flat against the face of the hedge. To ensure that you cut the top of a hedge level, insert a pole into the ground at each end and stretch a line tautly between them as a guideline.

The following plants are those most frequently used as hedges. The first list covers popular evergreen hedges and the second list includes well-known deciduous hedges. If your plant is not in either list, it may be in Chapter 3, Shrubs.

**TOP LEFT** *A correctly shaped hedge with the base wider than the top. The lower leaves benefit from available light and there is less chance of damage by heavy snow.*

**LEFT** *Hand shears are suitable for hedge plants with small leaves.*

**ABOVE** *Use pruners for large-leaved hedge plants so that leaf damage can be avoided.*

# POPULAR EVERGREEN HEDGES

**Aucuba japonica** (Japanese aucuba) Prune during late summer.

**Berberis x stenophylla** (Rosemary barberry) Trim during midsummer.

**Buxus sempervirens** (Common boxwood) Trim in late summer.

**Chamaecyparis lawsoniana** (False cypress) Prune in late spring.

**Cotoneaster lacteus** (Parvey cotoneaster, red clusterberry) Trim during summer.

**x Cupressocyparis leylandii** (Leyland cypress) Trim in late spring.

**Elaeagnus pungens 'Maculata'** (Variegated thorny eleagnus) Prune during late summer.

**Escallonia macrantha** (Red escallonia) Trim in spring and again after flowering.

**Euonymus japonicus** (Japanese spindle tree, evergreen euonymus) Prune in spring, and if growth has been vigorous, again in late summer.

**Griselinia littoralis** Prune in late summer.

**Hebe brachysiphon** Prune in late spring.

**Ilex aquifolium** (English holly) Trim during late summer.

**Lavandula spica** (English lavender) Trim in spring and again after flowering.

**Ligustrum ovalifolium** (California privet) Trim in spring, summer, and probably fall in most years.

**Lonicera nitida** (Box honeysuckle) Trim in spring and again during early fall.

**Olearia x haastii** (Daisy bush) Prune in late spring.

**Prunus lusitanica** (Cherry laurel, English laurel) Prune in spring.

**Pyracantha crenulata** (Firethorn) Trim in spring.

**Rhododendron ponticum** Prune when flowers fade in early summer.

**Rosmarinus officinalis** (Rosemary) Trim in spring.

**Santolina chamaecyparissus** (Lavender cotton) Trim in spring and again after flowering.

**Taxus baccata** (English yew) Trim in late spring.

**Thuja plicata** (Giant arbovitae) Trim in late spring.

**Weigela florida** Prune in late summer after flowering.

**BELOW** *Mixed hedges need careful selection to facilitate pruning; variegated plants alternated with green ones of the same species often work well together. Here* Chamaecyparis *is interplanted with its variegated form.*

# POPULAR DECIDUOUS HEDGES

**Berberis thunbergii** (Japanese barberry) Prune during late winter.

**Chaenomeles speciosa** (Japanese quince, flowering quince) Prune in spring, after flowering.

**Crataegus monogyna** (Hawthorn) Trim during late summer.

**Euonymus alatus** (Winged spindle tree) Prune in late summer.

**Fagus sylvatica** (European beech) Trim during late summer.

**Forsythia x intermedia** (Border forsythia) Trim once the flowers have faded.

**Fuchsia magellanica** (Magellan fuchsia, hardy fuchsia) Can be cut back hard if necessary during early spring.

**Hibiscus syriacus** Prune during spring.

**Hippophae rhamnoides** (Sallow thorn, common sea buckthorn) Prune in late summer.

**Philadelphus 'Manteau d'Hermine'** (Mock orange) Prune after flowering.

**Prunus cerasifera** (Cherry plum, myrobalan plum) Prune during early summer after flowering.

**Ribes sanguineum** (Flowering currant) Prune during very early spring, if it is straggly or has winter damage, and again after it flowers.

**Rosa rugosa** Thin out congested growth in late spring.

**Symphoricarpos albus** (Snowberry) Trim in late spring and midsummer.

**Syringa microphylla** (Littleleaf lilac) Prune in fall after flowering.

**Tamarix pentandra** (Tamarisk) Prune in spring.

**BELOW** *An evergreen hedge (Thuja) that has been clipped to form an archway into another part of the garden.*

**OVERLEAF** *Plants with small leaves are the best choice to train for topiary shapes.*

## THE ART OF TOPIARY

Topiary is an ancient art form which originated in Europe and was enthusiastically taken up by the Romans. In the modern world it appeals to people who want to add a touch of whimsy or a classic feature to their garden. Suitable plants, such as *Buxus* and *Taxus* can be clipped to an enormous variety of shapes: cones, pyramids, spirals, archways, pillars, seats, and even birds and animals.

If you live in an area regularly subject to snow and ice, choose a design with the shape tapering off at the top to minimize the possibility of damage. Even then, make sure you shake any snow off the plant before it settles too thickly.

The best trees and shrubs for topiary are those that are hardy, have small leaves, so that they don't have a ragged appearance after clipping, and are evergreen so that they retain their shape during winter. Plants that produce numerous dormant buds are always a good choice, because if a shoot dies back, there is a good chance it can be pruned back to a bud, which will grow out and fill the vacant space.

*Taxus* is one of the most commonly used plants for topiary training, as it meets all the necessary requirements. It is rather slow growing, but this has the advantage that you need to clip it less often to keep it in shape. *Buxus* is another favorite, and other suitable plants include *Ilex*, *Juniperus*, *Ligustrum*, *Pyracantha*, *Rosmarinus*, and a shrub that grows faster than most, *Lonicera nitida*. For whichever kind of plant you choose, you must first check that it is capable of withstanding regular clipping.

Single plants may be grown in containers or planted in the ground. You can grow two plants together to give added stability, or even more – for example, four to make the legs of an animal.

Lush growth is best avoided, since it will cause the plant to grow out of shape – so water sparingly; however, it is very important not to go to the other extreme and let a plant become dry at the roots. Feed occasionally with a general-purpose fertilizer. Sufficient light is necessary to maintain healthy, balanced growth, so that long, straggly shoots do not develop. Any stakes required to support the plant should, of course, be inserted before planting, to avoid root damage.

# CHAPTER SEVEN

# ORNAMENTAL TREES

**B**are-rooted trees, be they deciduous or evergreen, coniferous or nonconiferous, should be inspected as soon as they are received, and any damaged roots should be cut back to sound tissue. A container-grown tree is unlikely to have damaged roots, but it may well be root bound, with large roots circling the pot. If so, the roots should be carefully unwound and the planting hole should be made large enough so that they can be laid out flat, otherwise there is the risk that the roots will strangle one another as the plant grows and will not provide the tree with a stable anchorage.

## DECIDUOUS AND NONCONIFEROUS EVERGREEN TREES

Trim long shoots by a quarter after planting. This is particularly important with evergreens, since the amount of foliage on long shoots is likely to make

too great a demand on the tree's resources until it has established a good root system. If the leaves cannot get enough water and nourishment they may dry up completely, resulting in the death of the tree.

Once you have trimmed the tree, keep the soil around the roots moist; this helps the tree to recover, thus avoiding the need for too much pruning. It is also a good idea to spray the leaves occasionally with clear water except during periods of bright sunshine, when the foliage may be scorched. If this is not possible, it is worth spraying the foliage with a ready-made solution you can buy that reduces moisture loss to the air.

**TOP** *Trees with varied shapes, and in a mix of evergreen, deciduous, and coniferous, make an interesting collection.*

**LEFT** *The bright leaves and stems of* Acer palmatum *are enhanced by removing those that have died back.*

**TO REMOVE OR NOT TO REMOVE LATERALS ON A TREE**

**1** When the lateral growth is kept on a young tree, the tree increases its girth faster than when it is removed.

**2** When laterals are pruned away the trunk stays thinner but grows taller faster.

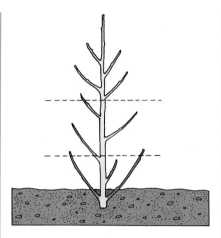

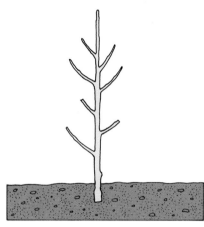

**3** A compromise is often the best course to take concerning laterals: remove laterals on the lower third of the trunk, shorten the laterals on the middle portion to three buds, and retain the lateral growth on the upper third of the trunk.

**When to prune**

Generally, deciduous trees are best pruned just before the sap rises in spring (provided severe frost is not expected); otherwise they may bleed. (Certain trees, such as *Betula* and *Acer* are inclined to lose a considerable amount of sap when cut at other times of the year.) It has been suggested, however, that wounds heal more quickly when the tree is in full leaf, because gumming of the sap-conducting tissue and callus formation over the wound is brought about more quickly. It is also claimed that air-borne disease spores likely to attack an open wound are less numerous during hot, dry weather. Pruning before sap rises, during the dormant season, induces vigor in the plant,

though it should also be taken into account that it may well reduce that year's flowering and fruiting. If these are more important to you than the tree's vigor, you can delay pruning until the summer.

Nonconiferous, evergreen trees should be pruned during early and mid-spring, as and when necessary.

**TRAINING**

There is a great sense of satisfaction in training a young tree that, given the opportunity and depending on species, may grow for decades or even hundreds of years.

**Lateral growth**

On both grafted and nongrafted trees, laterals will develop. If you keep them, the main stem will thicken at the expense of height; if you remove them, the main stem will remain thin but grow taller than it would otherwise have done. The best approach is a compromise. Remove all lateral growth from the bottom third of the main stem during the dormant season. On the middle third, reduce laterals to three buds. Leave the upper third unpruned, unless a double leader develops, in which case cut the weaker shoot out.

**Standard trees**

Pruning during the following two years depends on the type of tree. A standard – a tree with a trunk clear of laterals up to approximately 6½ft (2m) – is the best choice for a small garden. Allow an intended standard to grow up to about 7ft (2.25m); then cut growth back to firm wood just before the sap rises in spring. Any secondary growth from the lowest third of the trunk should be cut away. At the end of the two years, when the plant has become well established, all laterals from the middle third of the main stem should be removed, allowing a good crown to develop.

Once a standard tree is mature, little pruning should be necessary except to remove dead or crossing branches and any laterals that develop lower than the desired crown. Strong water sprouts arising from previously cut areas should be removed completely. Any branches extending too far can be cut back to a suitable sublateral (growth arising from a lateral). Old wood is best removed each winter to stimulate young replacement shoots.

### Larger trees

Where space is available to grow a large specimen, the bare portion of trunk can be extended to 8½ft (2.5m) or more. Taller trunks can be especially effective on trees such as *Nyssa sylvatica* that tend to have lower branches which curve down to the ground as they mature. On all grafted trees shoots arising as suckers should be removed at an early stage.

Unless a weeping tree has already undergone formative pruning, cut the leader and lateral shoots back to two or three buds each winter until the tree reaches the desired height. With trees that do not produce a vertical leader naturally, it will be necessary to tie the leading shoot to the supporting stake.

When training a tree into a shape such as a column or pyramid, do not remove laterals from low down on the main stem, unless they are overcrowded, damaged, or crossing.

### GENERAL MAINTENANCE PRUNING

Wood should be removed from a mature tree with care and consideration for its shape. For example, it is often better to take out an unwanted branch completely, rather than cut it back, otherwise the shortened branch may well produce a lateral that will simply replace the original branch.

If a tree is lop-sided, cut the lateral shoots on the weak side back hard to within two or three buds and prune the strong side only lightly. Vertical shoots competing with the leader should be shortened or removed. On a tree that produces a large amount of short-stemmed, congested growth, especially towards the center of the plant, thin out this growth to allow air to circulate and light to penetrate.

Once formative pruning has been completed, deciduous and nonconiferous evergreen trees require comparatively little in the way of maintenance to keep them looking attractive.

**SHAPING A WEEPING TREE**

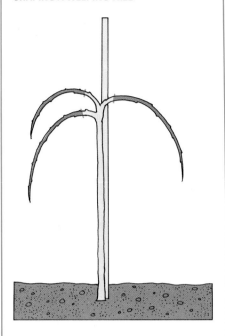

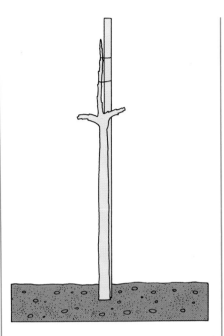

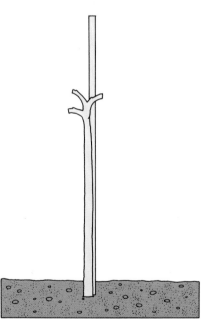

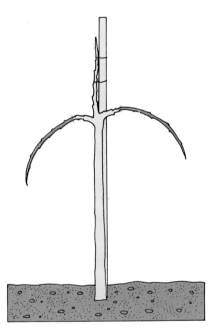

**1** Cut the leader and the lateral shoots back to two or three buds every winter until the tree has reached a suitable height.

**2** If there is no obvious leader, drive a stake next to the tree and tie the longest middle shoot to it. Continue to prune back the shoots until the tree has reached the desired height.

**RESHAPING A LOPSIDED TREE**

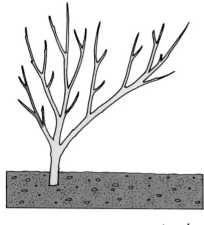

**1** First, hard prune the lateral shoots on the side that is weakest by cutting them back to two or three buds. Lightly prune the strong side.

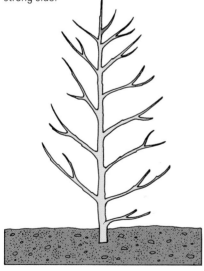

**2** As the tree grows, prune any vertical shoots that compete with the leader.

# POPULAR DECIDUOUS AND NONCONIFEROUS EVERGREEN TREES

The more exact seasonal pruning times given in the list, such as early fall or late spring, are not to be taken as hard-and-fast rules. Use them rather as guides, since seasonal changes can vary from year to year and, in addition, conditions vary in different parts of the country.

**Acacia** On mature trees occasional thinning is all that is necessary.

**Acer** (Maple) If the young tree develops a double leader, remove the weaker of the two immediately. Cut out dead wood and congested branches in early fall, when the sap flow is slowing down.

**Aesculus** (Horse chestnut, buckeye) Prune in late winter by removing congested growth. Cut away lower branches intermittently as the tree grows, until it reaches a height of 11½ft (3.5m).

**Ailanthus** (Tree of heaven) These trees are prone to suckering when heavily pruned. Remove suckers, together with damaged or congested wood, in winter.

**Albizia** Winter-damaged wood should be removed during spring. If the entire crown is affected, the plant can be cut down to ground level to shoot up the following growing season.

**Alnus** (Alder) The only pruning necessary is to remove weak and congested growth.

**Amelanchier** (Serviceberry, shad bush) Suckers on these small trees need removing as soon as they appear. Cut out any misplaced branches and congested growth in winter.

**Arbutus** (Manzanita, strawberry tree) Remove any damaged wood as soon as possible, cutting back to a sound lateral. Suckers should be removed at an early stage.

**Arctostaphylos** (Bearberry, manganita) Enhance the reddish color of the tree bark by thinning out growth during spring. Cut out any winter damage at the same time.

**Azara** Carry out maintenance pruning and dead-heading after flowering in early summer.

**Betula** (Birch) Dead, twiggy branches are liable to be shed and, unless removed, will congest the tree. Young growth is susceptible to decay, so do not prune more than is strictly necessary. Overcrowded growth is best cut out during late fall and early winter when the flow of sap has slowed.

**Carpinus** (Hornbeam, ironwood) The only pruning required is the removal of dead or congested wood in winter.

**Castanea** (Chestnut) Remove water sprouts and any weak or congested growth during winter. Old trees tend to shed large limbs, so it is advisable to have them inspected by qualified tree surgeons from time to time.

**Celtis** (Hackberry) Carry out maintenance pruning in winter or early spring.

**Cercidiphyllum** Trees with multi-trunks may require thinning in late fall.

**Cladrastis** (Yellowwood) Periodically remove the very large limbs likely to be shed.

**Cornus** (Dogwood) Occasional maintenance pruning after flowers fade in late spring is all that is necessary.

**Corylus (Hazel)** Prune hard during the formative years so that a spur system develops. Then maintenance prune and remove suckers.

**Crataegus (Hawthorn)** Multistemmed trees are considered to be more attractive than those with a single trunk. Do any necessary thinning during winter

**ABOVE** *A pyramidal* Nyssa sylvatica.

and remove suckers as soon as you notice them.

**Davidia** Since these trees are slow to heal cuts, pruning (normally done in winter) should be carried out only when absolutely necessary.

**Elaeagnus** Normally grown as shrubs, these plants can be trained to make single-trunked small trees. Remove suckers promptly. Any maintenance pruning should be done in early summer after flowers fade.

**Eucalyptus** Maintenance prune during early summer. If you prefer the juvenile leaf form, cut stems back to the main framework at the same time.

**Euonymus** (Spindle tree) Maintenance prune during spring. To encourage beautiful colors on plants noted for their fall foliage, prune hard to promote more vigorous growth.

**Fraxinus** (Ash) The wood is brittle and therefore susceptible to snow loading and wind. For this reason wide crotches are to be encouraged by removing the weaker leader at an early stage in the plant's training. Remove water sprouts and carry out other maintenance pruning in spring.

**Gleditsia** (Honey locust) Some trees produce narrow crotches; correct this by removing the weaker shoot at an early stage.

**Hamamelis** See Shrubs.

**Ilex** (Holly) Maintenance prune during winter. Cut back to a bud or healthy branch, since replacement growth is unlikely to arise from the trunk.

**Jacaranda** These trees are subject to the disease die-back, so remove dead wood as soon as you notice it.

**x Laburnocytisus** Remove the shoots producing yellow flowers at flowering time when they are easily detected.

**Leptospermum** (Tea tree) During late spring remove congested growth and cut back branches to maintain the tree's shape.

**Liriodendron** (Tulip tree) Any wounds are slow to heal, so pruning, which is best done during late summer, should be carried out only when strictly necessary; smooth rough cuts to assist healing.

**Magnolia** Deciduous trees should be pruned only to remove damaged branches, since the wood is slow to heal; do this in early summer. Prune evergreen trees in early fall by removing old branches, which will encourage replacements.

**Malus** (Flowering crab apple) Mature trees will need thinning occasionally by cutting congested spurs back to strong lateral shoots. The best time to prune and to remove any suckers growing from the rootstock is during early spring.

**Mespilus** (Medlar) Remove crossing branches and low ones that touch the ground, as well as congested growth, during late winter.

**Morus** (Mulberry) Maintenance pruning should be carried out in winter.

**Myoporum** In late spring remove winter-damaged shoots and carry out maintenance pruning.

**Nyssa** (Sour gum) Maintenance pruning should be done when the brightly colored leaves have fallen in fall.

**Olearia** See Shrubs.

**Osmanthus** See Shrubs.

**Ostrya** (Hop hornbeam) These trees are liable to bleed badly due to strong root pressure, so carry out any maintenance pruning during late fall or in the winter months.

**Paulownia** Remove winter damage in spring and any congested growth after flowering in early summer.

**Populus** (Poplar, aspen, cottonwood) These very vigorous trees should be

pruned during fall when the flow of sap is reduced, otherwise severe bleeding may result.

**Prunus** (Flowering plum, cherry, almond) Prune as necessary to thin growth. Since the trees are prone to silverleaf disease, prune during summer so that wounds heal quickly. Remove any suckers promptly.

**Quercus** (Oak) Foliage on evergreen trees that has been scorched by wind or frost should be trimmed away in late spring.

**Rhus** (Sumac) A painful allergy can result from coming into contact with the sap of these plants, so wear gardening gloves when carrying out pruning. Thin trees during winter and remove any suckers.

**Robinia** (Locust) Die-back is common on these trees; remove dead wood as soon as possible to prevent necria canker. Watch out for damaged branches since the wood is very brittle.

**Salix** (Willow, osier) Since these trees are inclined to bleed badly during winter and spring, any pruning should be carried out during late summer and fall. Removal of suckers and water shoots is most important. Thin out overgrown plants by removing branches. Despite possible bleeding, trees grown for winter colored bark should be pollarded in late spring.

**Sparmannia** (Linden) Remove winter damage during spring. The plant will regenerate from hard pruning.

**Syringa** See Shrubs.

**Tamarix** (Tamarisk) Usually grown as shrubs, these plants can be trained as small trees by removing suckers to establish one main stem. Subsequently, thin out side shoots to form a permanent framework.

**Ulmus** (Elm) Cut off and destroy diseased wood and damaged and congested growth. This is best done in fall.

**Umbellularia** Winter damage and any growth spreading beyond its allotted space should be removed during spring.

**Vitex** See Shrubs.

**ABOVE** *Standard trees like this Prunus yedoensis are more appropriate for the larger garden.*

**BELOW** *Some plants are grown especially for their decorative stems, and in this case hard pruning to produce water shoots is desirable, as with this Salix 'Vitellina'.*

# POPULAR CONIFERS

Conifers grown alone require scarcely any pruning, and those fitted into a border or hedge need mere trimming, cutting back as little as possible. The reason is that, with the exception of yew, conifers are unlikely to carry dormant buds on mature wood and consequently will not regenerate when cut back hard.

Spring is the best time to prune most conifers that require treatment, although damaged branches should of course be cut back or removed as soon as possible. Conifers generally have one leader; if double leaders appear, remove the weaker shoot in spring, cutting back to the main stem. In the case of plants that produce a multihead naturally, leave all the leaders in place and tie the plant in to prevent snow and wind damage (see Chapter 1).

**Abies** (Fir) These trees can be modified in shape to a more compact and attractive form by reducing the length of the "candles," the new shoots that appear at the growth tips. Snap rather than cut them away to avoid damaging the needles. The central leader of a young plant may be severed by animals or the wind, and if this happens a lateral branch lower down the main stem should be tied vertically to a stake as a replacement leader.

Branches that are spoiling the shape of the tree by growing too large may be cut back to a bud or lateral shoot during late winter or early spring.

**Araucaria araucana** (Monkey puzzle) In spring pinch back the side shoots lightly to maintain the desired shape. Do not remove the central leader, otherwise the plant will lose its attractive shape. The lower branches may eventually touch the ground, in which case they should be lopped back to the main trunk.

**Cedrus** (Cedar) Young plants are inclined to produce double leaders, and the weaker of these should be removed

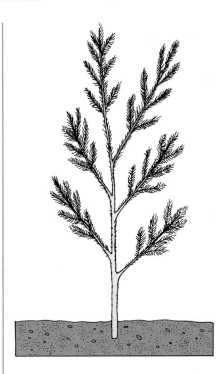

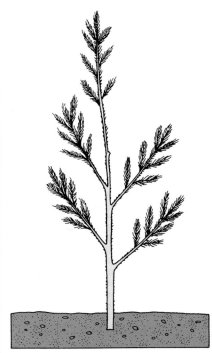

**ABOVE** This conifer developed a double leader, or two head shoots. To keep its proper shape the weaker shoot is removed in spring.

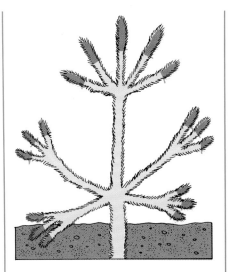

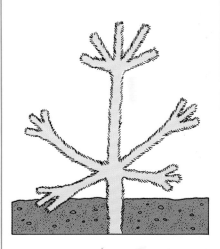

**ABOVE** New shoots at the growing tips of firs and some other conifers are called candles, because that is what they look like. Snap them off, rather than cut them, to keep trees compact.

during spring. In late summer, to shape the young plant, lightly cut back the current season's growth to a bud or side shoot. Mature trees may need to be thinned occasionally at the same time of year; either cut branches back to a lateral or remove them completely.

**Chamaecyparis** (False cypress) Most large trees of this genus require little pruning, apart from perhaps removing a competitive leader during the early stages of growth. Trees that lack vigor can be encouraged to grow more strongly by cutting back the current season's growth by one-third during late summer. Dwarf trees can be trained to remain compact by occasionally pinching back the current season's growth.

**Pinus** (Pine) Bearing in mind that these conifers do not produce growth from old wood; a mature branch should be removed only with special care. Plants are best pruned in spring, just as growth is commencing. Pinch back the new candles by half. If a new shoot needs to be reduced further, the complete candle may be removed, but take care to avoid removing the whole candle cluster, otherwise no further growth will develop from that area.

**Taxus** (Yew) Since these trees will regenerate from old wood, old branches can be thinned when necessary in spring, with the confidence of knowing that any gap will be filled by new growth. Plants can be clipped to retain their shape.

**LEFT** Chamaeyoparis lawsoniana *'Kilmacurragh'; this is a tall example of the columnar shape.*

**ABOVE** *The* Taxus baccata *(yew) hedge is wider at the top and prone to damage by snow.*

**Ginkgo** Keep pruning to a minimum for this slow-growing tree, which does not easily heal; only remove badly placed shoots.

**Juniperus** (Juniper) If a plant is outgrowing its allotted space, it can be brought back to a more manageable size by cutting some side shoots back to the main branches in early spring; these side shoots need to be selected carefully since new growth will not arise from old wood. Shoots on the current season's growth may be cut back by half during late summer to control the size of a tree. Prostrate forms tend to send up vertical shoots from time to time. These should be cut back in summer to the point where they arise.

# CHAPTER EIGHT

# FRUIT AND NUT TREES

**LEFT** *Discovery – a good early dessert apple.*

F ruit and nut trees require a good deal of attention when it comes to pruning. This is especially true during the first years after planting, which are so important in determining the future health and fruiting capability of the tree. With that in mind, it is usually best to purchase a three-year-old tree, since it will already have received most of its formative training. Such a tree may well be growing in a container, in which case there will be only a minimal check to growth when it is planted.

The sections that immediately follow describe pruning and training the most common home garden fruit trees – apples and pears. However, much of what is found here can be applied to other types of fruit (and nut) trees, as noted in the sections on other fruits and nuts, later in this chapter.

## PRUNING STAGES FOR APPLES AND PEARS

From the pruning aspect, the lifespan of a fruit tree can be divided into three main stages. The first is the formative stage, when hard pruning gives the best results, though at the expense of delaying cropping. During the second stage

light pruning is carried out to encourage fruit bud development. And in the third stage pruning varies in severity as necessary, to bring about balanced growth.

During stage one, which lasts for the first four years of the tree's life, strong growth is needed so that enough vigorous shoots are formed to build up the main framework. Prune hard in winter by cutting the previous season's growth back to within a few inches of its base.

Pruning is less severe in the second stage, to enable the tree to bear fruit. In winter, on trees that bear their fruit entirely on spurs, lightly tip the extension shoot at the end of branch leaders. On tip-bearing varities (those that produce fruit buds at the tips of shoots as well as on spurs), or for trees that are growing vigorously, do not prune the extension shoots. Remove any laterals growing towards the center of the tree.

During the third stage, the aim of pruning is to maintain a balance between cropping and growth. In winter prune trees that are growing and cropping satisfactorily by shortening extension shoots and cutting back laterals fairly close to their bases.

### Weak or over-vigorous growth

Sometimes a tree will produce an abnormally large crop and very little extension growth during the year. In that case, prune severely during the following winter: cut back the extension shoot on each branch leader to within a few inches of the base and shorten all laterals and spur clusters crowded with fruit buds.

During a year when a tree crops lightly – either due to lack of fruit buds, late frost, or bird damage – it will probably produce over-vigorous growth. You may remedy the problem simply by doing very little pruning the following winter. If, however, the tree continues to make strong growth, it will be necessary to undertake summer pruning (see the section "Cordons" in this chapter), bark ringing, or root pruning (see Chapter 1). You can also moderate vigorous growth by reducing the amount of nitrogen in the annual dressing of fertilizer you give or by allowing grass to grow beneath the tree.

### Overgrown trees

Old trees that have become overgrown are difficult to manage, and it is often necessary to reduce their height by pruning the main branches. This should be done in winter by cutting back the branches to smaller ones that have a strong shoot of the previous season's growth. Very old trees, however, should be cut back gradually over three or four years; sudden, severe pruning could prove fatal.

Branches that have produced a heavy crop are inclined to bend downward; remove those touching the ground to prevent fruit from becoming soiled.

**ABOVE** *Remove branches that are touching the ground to prevent the fruit from becoming spoiled.*

## TRAINING APPLE AND PEAR TREES

Before you can begin training a young fruit tree, it is necessary to be able to distinguish between fruit buds and growth buds. The time of year to see the difference is winter: fruit buds are large and rounded, whereas growth buds are smaller and pointed and tend to be flattened against the stem.

There are a number of different ways you can choose to train your apple or pear tree, depending on how much space you have, how much time you can devote to pruning, and personal preference as to form. The most common form is the open-center bush, followed by the dwarf pyramid. A form that is both highly productive and highly attractive is the fan-trained tree. This, however, takes up a great deal of wall space, and for a small garden, cordons are a good solution.

**BELOW** *Dwarf pyramid trees are easily managed.*

**ABOVE** A fruit tree that looks like the top drawing is overgrown and should be pruned as shown to make it more manageable.

## THE OPEN-CENTER, BUSH-SHAPED FRUIT TREE

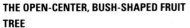

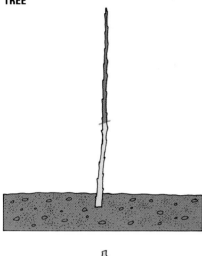

This is the general shape of the open-center bush, the style that is most suitable for home gardens.

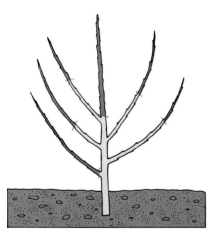

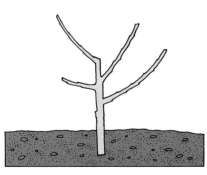

**1** The first step in training is to cut the stem during its first winter after planting to just above a bud, approximately 2ft (60cm) from the ground. It is a good idea then to nick the bud to encourage the growth of good branches below it.

**2** The next winter, cut off the new top shoot down to the branch right below it. Prune off all but three or four well-spaced young branches and shorten them by half to an outward-facing bud.
**3** The third winter prune some of the laterals that have since developed on the three or four branches, and cut back the rest of the laterals to three or four buds.

## Open-center bush trees

The open-center bush is suitable for most home orchards. The shape is good for both apple and pear trees, although the latter are slightly more difficult to train. A tree pruned as an open-center bush remains a reasonable height, so that pruning, harvesting, and, if necessary, spraying can be carried out fairly easily. It is possible to buy trees which have already been trained to shape by the nursery, but you can train a tree yourself by buying a one-year-old specimen consisting of a single stem growing from the rootstock.

The first step is to cut the stem to just above a bud about 2ft (60cm) from the ground during the first winter. What is required is that the topmost bud will produce a branch growing out at an angle. To prevent the possibility of the bud being too vigorous and producing an almost vertical shoot, you can nick it (as explained in Chapter 1). This will reduce its vigor, to the benefit of the buds below, which should then produce good branches growing at a suitable angle.

The following winter remove the top shoot, which has grown from the nicked bud, cutting it back to the young branch below. Retain three or four of the young branches that have developed, ensuring that they are well spaced around the one-year-old stem. These will form the main framework of the tree. Shorten them by half to an outward-facing bud.

During the third winter cut back by half some of the laterals arising from the branches (these will form the next stage of the main framework) and prune the remainder back to three or four buds. The number of laterals to retain as part of the framework will depend on the size of the tree and the type of growth made: ideally, the tips of the framework laterals should be 1½ft (45cm) apart after pruning.

## Pruning to encourage fruiting – method 1

The tree will now have reached the stage when lighter pruning is necessary to encourage fruiting. A method that has been used successfully for many years (and has been used in the author's own fruit garden) is known as the renewal system. This encourages wide spacing of the branches to allow new generations of growth to replace that which has borne fruit.

Close examination of a mature branch will reveal that the current season's extension has growth buds; that the previous year's wood contains fruit buds and a lateral shoot; and that three-year-old wood has developed two-year-old lateral shoots, which have in turn produced one-year-old sub-laterals. Each year remove a proportion of the old wood to give space to younger growth. The actual amount of wood you prune away will depend on the vigor and fruiting history of the tree.

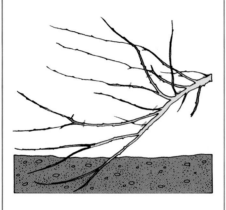

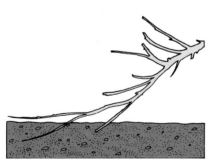

**ABOVE** After the formative pruning of the first 4 years, lighter pruning to maintain fruiting follows. Method one, the renewal system, involves removing a proportion of old wood each year. Some branches on slow-growing trees should be pruned by half. Vigorous trees need lighter pruning; cut back older wood and competing branches but leave a number of the laterals uncut each year. Ultimately, branch leaders should be about 1ft (30cm) apart on a mature tree. This close-up of one branch shows about how much wood to prune away.

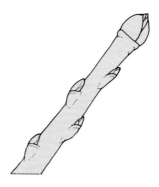

**ABOVE** Note the thicker, rounder fruit (or blossom) bud at the tip of this leader, compared to the smaller growth buds along the branch.

On plants that are not making sufficient growth, reduce some branches by half, cutting them back to an upward-growing lateral.

A tree that has a good balance between fruit and growth should be pruned to leave a number of lateral shoots uncut each year. Cut some of the wood that has borne fruit back to a replacement lateral that has been pulled down into position by the weight of crops. When two shoots are competing as branch leaders, either remove the weaker entirely or cut it back to three buds to produce a fruiting spur. Ideally, branch leaders should be 1ft (30cm) apart from each other on a mature tree.

Certain varieties of apple produce fruit (or blossom) buds at the tips of some leaders. These tip bearers may still be grown by the renewal system, but try to prune only those shoots with growth buds at the tip, leaving the majority of shoots with fruit buds to develop blossom.

### Pruning to encourage fruiting — method 2

There is an alternative method to the renewal system which retains the branches for a longer time. Shorten the leader by a half, and encourage fruiting spurs to develop by cutting each year's lateral extension growth back to three or four buds and sub-laterals back to one bud. Sooner or later a congested spur system will develop; at that point remove some spurs completely and thin others out.

Here is another pruning approach (method two) that encourages fruiting but does not prune branches so heavily.

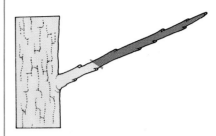

**1** Each year's laterals are cut back to three or four buds.

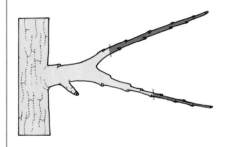

**2** The sub-laterals are cut back to one bud.

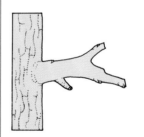

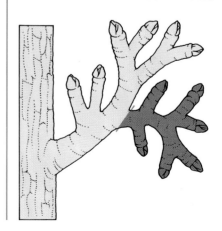

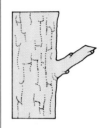

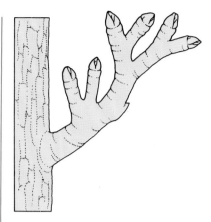

**3** The congested spur system that develops should be thinned out when necessary.

## Dwarf pyramids

The dwarf pyramid fruit tree is approximately the same height as the open-center bush, except that the branches grow on an extended main stem called the central leader. Train this type of tree by first cutting the one-year-old main stem back to 2½ft (75cm) in the winter after planting. The following winter cut the subsequent vigorous terminal shoot back by half and cut four or five of the shoots growing from the central leader back to a bud on the underside of the shoot, approximately 6in (15cm) from the base. In summer cut back those laterals that aren't contributing to the main pyramid shape to four or five leaves.

During the following winter shorten the extended terminal shoot by half again and cut the extension shoots of the original tier of branches back to a downward-facing bud 6in (15cm) from the base of the shoot. In summer prune as during the previous summer.

To encourage fruiting when the tree has reached its required height, use one of the two pruning systems recommended for open-center bush trees.

**THE DWARF PYRAMID**

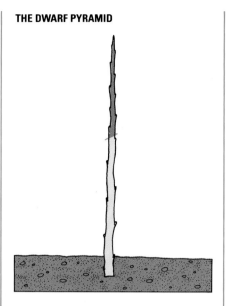

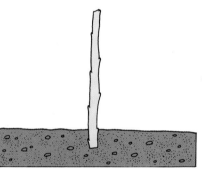

**1** In the first winter after planting cut back the main stem to 2½ft (75cm).

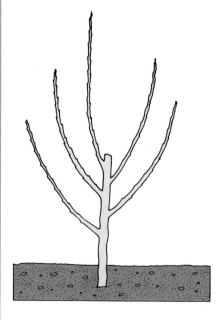

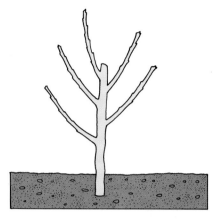

**2** The next winter cut back by half the main terminal shoot and also cut back four or five of the shoots growing from the central leader to a downward-growing bud that is about 6in (15cm) from the base.

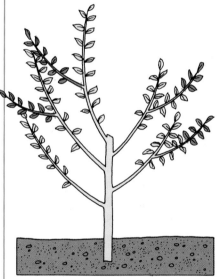

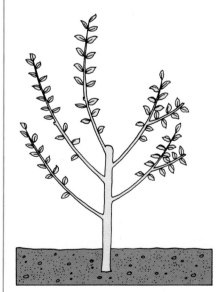

**3** That summer cut back less significant laterals to four or five leaves.

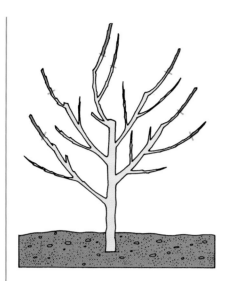

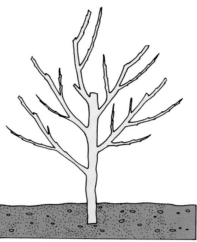

**4** The next winter prune similarly to the winter before by cutting back the extended terminal shoot by half again and cutting the extension shoots of the original branches back to a downward-facing bud 6in (15cm) from the base. The next summer prune as the summer before. In following years use a pruning method that encourages fruiting as for open-center bush trees.

**ABOVE** *Regrowth after summer pruning should be cut back to one bud.*

## Cordons

With both apple and pear trees you need to plant at least two varieties close together so that cross-pollination can take place to produce a worthwhile crop. If space for growing fruit trees is restricted in your garden, the cordon system of training is ideal. The trees are grown 3ft (1m) apart, with the main stem growing at an angle to the ground and supported by a bamboo cane fixed to horizontal wires stretched between posts. Growing the tree at an angle helps to reduce its vigor, which encourages earlier cropping and reduces extension growth.

Initially the main stem is trained at an angle of 45 degrees to the ground. Do not prune it unless growth is weak, in which case the current season's growth should be cut back; the extent of pruning will depend on the amount of vigor required. Once the main stem has reached the desired height, untie it from its support and secure it again at a reduced angle.

Each summer prune the laterals by reducing the current season's growth to five leaves. Do this in late summer when the base of the shoot is ripe; new growth will emerge if you prune too early. If this should happen, pinch back subsequent growth to one leaf. In winter cut laterals back to two or three buds to form a spur system.

### PRUNING CORDONS

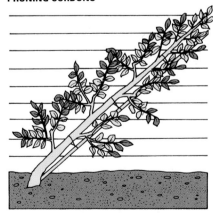

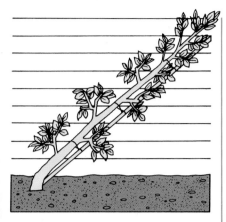

**1** Summer pruning is carried out each year on the laterals by reducing the current season's growth to five leaves.

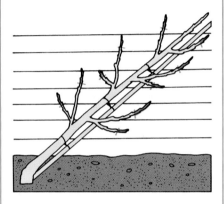

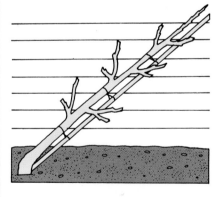

**2** Winter pruning consists of pruning the laterals back to two or three buds to form a spur system.

## Fan-trained trees

Trees trained in this way can be both productive and ornamental. During the first winter after planting, shorten the one-year-old main stem to 2ft (60cm). At the level of the top of the plant secure two bamboo canes to horizontal wires, each at an angle of 45 degrees, so that they form a 'V'. The following summer, when shoots have grown from the foremost opposite buds, carefully tie each to one of the canes with garden string to form a Y-shaped tree. Remove all other shoots and buds.

During the second winter shorten the two shoots to 1½ft (45cm). In summer tie the extension growth from the tip of each shoot to canes at the same angle as the growth; choose two evenly spaced sub-laterals on each shoot, one growing upward, the other downward, and tie them to additional canes; and prune away the remaining shoots and buds on the original two shoots.

During the following winter shorten the sub-laterals to 2ft (60cm). In summer tie in subsequent extension growth to canes; choose two evenly spaced sub-sub-laterals – again one upward-growing shoot and one downward-growing – and tie them in to canes. Then remove other shoots and buds.

Formative training is now complete. Subsequently the only winter pruning required is to remove congested spurs to allow room for replacement growth to be tied to canes. Summer prune each year when the base of the current season's growth is ripe. Once growth has become woody, remove the canes and tie the growth to the wires.

**ABOVE** *A fan-trained apple tree with laterals spread out and tied to wires.*

**TRAINING FAN-SHAPED TREES**

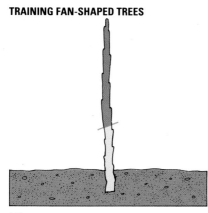

**1** The first year after planting cut back the one-year-old stem to 2ft (60cm) tall.

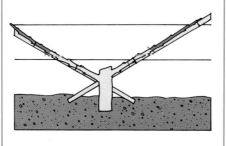

**2** The following summer tie bamboo canes to the horizontal wires at 45-degree angles

to them; then tie the two shoots that have grown from the foremost opposite buds in the stem to these canes. Remove all other shoots and buds.

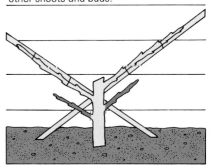

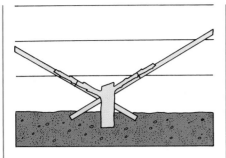

**3** The second winter reduce the two shoots to 18in (45cm).

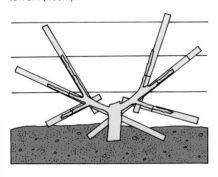

**4** In the second summer, tie extension growth from the tip of each shoot to canes; again choose two sub-laterals on each stem as before and tie them to canes.

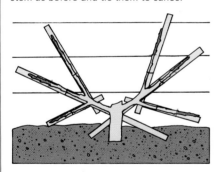

**5** During the third winter, shorten sub-laterals to 2ft (60cm).

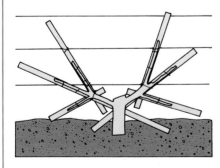

**6** The third summer sees subsequent extension growth tied to canes; again one sub-lateral above and one below.

**RIGHT** *Espalier lateral shoots are trained at right angles to the main stem.*

## Espaliers

An espalier consists of a main stem with lateral branches trained at right angles to it along wires. Immediately after planting a one-year-old tree, cut it back to a bud 14in (35cm) from the ground. Leave a second and third bud, one on each side of the stem, and rub off the remainder. Steady, uniform growth is required from all three buds, so notch the lowest bud (which otherwise may not be vigorous enough) as described in Chapter 1. During the following summer tie the shoot that grows from the top bud to a vertical cane attached to wires, and tie the other two to canes, at a 45-degree angle to the wires, as for a fan-trained tree.

The following winter untie the side shoots from the canes and tie them horizontally to the wires. Shorten each by approximately half, depending on its vigor: strong growth will need less severe pruning, weak growth more. Cut the extension shoot on the main stem back to a bud approximately 2in (5cm) above the second wire (the one above that supporting the first two laterals); then select two opposite buds as before and notch the lower.

The following summer tie the resultant shoots in to canes as for the first tier of laterals. Tie the extension growth of the first tier to its wire. Summer prune as before. In late fall prune any secondary growth arising from the cut sub-laterals by pinching it back to one leaf. That winter prune leaders as before and select buds for the next tier.

In succeeding years add further tiers until you have the number you require; then rub off any new, unwanted buds to keep the tree to the desired size and shape.

# OTHER FRUIT AND NUT TREES

**Almond** Training during the early years is as for apples and pears, except that you should prune during spring rather than in the dormant season. This is so that cuts heal quickly and lessen the chances of silver leaf disease attacking the plant.

Prune mature trees in summer when necessary, by cutting out congested spurs flush with the branch. You may also need to open up the center of the tree from time to time so that light and air can penetrate; but avoid hard pruning, or strong, unproductive water sprouts may develop. However, an exception can be made in the case of a very old tree, which can be rejuvenated by dehorning: cutting old wood back to substantial lateral branches.

**Apricot** In cold climates the plants are best fan-trained on a south-facing wall, since flowers appear during early spring, when they are susceptible to late frosts. Prune in summer, following the recommendations for peaches. Apricot trees are inclined to be vigorous and, although summer pruning and stopping are usually sufficient, they sometimes require root pruning.

The plant is often grown as a free-standing tree in warm climates. Since most of the fruit is borne on spurs which, ideally, are replaced from time to time, a training and pruning system similar to the renewal system for apples is satisfactory.

Unfortunately, the apricot is very prone to the diseases die-back and gummosis. To avoid these, large pruning cuts should be kept to a minimum. However, old, unproductive trees can be rejuvenated by spreading dehorning over two or three years (see Almond).

**Avocado** This is a large tree that will grow only in warm, wet climates where there is a minimum temperature of 26°C (79°F) and a minimum annual rainfall of 2½ft (75cm). To keep the height and spread of the tree within bounds, shorten branches; occasionally

**TRAINING A HALF-STANDARD CHERRY TREE**

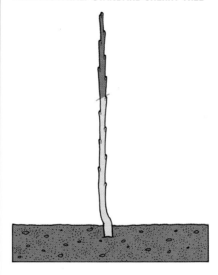

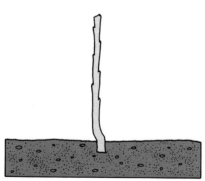

**1** Cut back the one-year-old plant to 5ft (1.5m) in late spring after planting.

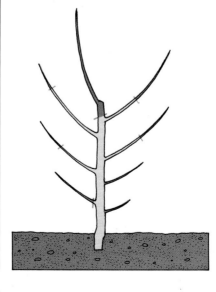

**2** During the second spring, cut back halfway four of the new branches; choose those that are growing at a nice, wide angle to the main stem. Remove any other branches.

**3** The following spring, tip back two or three of the laterals that have grown from the shoots that were pruned the year before; tip back to outward-facing buds.

thin out congested growth; and remove any dead branches.

**Cherry, acid** This tree is not as vigorous as the sweet cherry and so is more suitable for the smaller garden. Prune fan-trained trees in the same way as for peach trees, apart from spacing the side shoots 2in (5cm) apart. Each spring remove some of the wood that is two or more years old, taking care to leave alone the previous season's growth, since this bears the fruit. However, one-year-old wood that is congested can also be removed.

Train free-standing bushes in the same way as for plums. Cut out some of the old wood each year to avoid congested growth, paying particular attention to the center of the tree.

**Cherry, sweet** Plants are prone to silver leaf disease, so prune in spring, when growth is just beginning, or, in the case of mature plants, in summer, after fruiting.

To train a half-standard (which is simply a tree that is shorter than a standard), cut the stem of a one-year-old plant back to 5ft (1.5m) in late spring after planting. During the second spring, select four branches growing at a wide angle to the main stem and shorten them by half. Remove the remaining shoots, cutting them back to the main stem. During the third spring, cut back the tip of two or three laterals (or more if there are more of them) arising from each branch to an outward-facing bud.

Train fan-trained sweet cherry trees in basically the same way as peach trees. When shoots reach the limit of their boundary, shorten them to a lateral. As with other fan-trained plants, it is best to remove the shoots growing inward or away from the plant at an early stage; pinch other shoots at the fifth leaf stage.

**BELOW** *Cherries can be fan-trained like peaches.*

**ABOVE** *Free-standing cherry bushes can be trained in the same way as plums. This is a Morello cherry bush.*

To reduce the possibility of silver leaf disease, it is best to complete pruning in early fall: remove dead wood and shorten shoots already pinched to five leaves back to three. Tie in replacement shoots, tying the strong growers horizontally to reduce vigor.

**Citrus** The orange and lemon family will fruit satisfactorily outdoors only in warm climates. Training consists simply of restricting the young tree's height to approximately 3ft (1m) and lightly tipping the laterals by about 2in (5cm). Once trained, the only pruning necessary is to thin out overcrowded shoots in summer so that branches do not touch one another. Do not prune mature plants more than is absolutely necessary.

Lemon trees tend to be vigorous, and fruit is often borne toward the end of long shoots. To moderate this vigor pinch back new growth during the active growing period to encourage shorter stems and a more substantial framework.

Citrus plants are prone to send up suckers from the rootstock. Remove them at an early stage.

**Filbert and hazel** Cut the main stem back to three or four buds after planting; then cut growth that develops from these buds back to three or four outward-facing buds. Prune in this way each year until the tree has reached a height of 6½ft (2m). By this time the main framework will have been established and nuts will be borne on laterals each year.

The male catkins grow early in the year on wood produced during the previous growing season; the small red female flowers, from which the nuts will develop, are borne on wood of the same age or older. Prune in late spring when the pollen has been dispersed. Cut back vigorous side shoots to a catkin a few inches from the base of the shoot. Cut spent wood that produced nuts the previous year back to three buds and remove some old wood to avoid congestion. Retain the previous year's growth. In late summer snap off vigorous side shoots 6in (15cm) from their base to encourage fruit spurs to develop.

**Fig** Fan-training against a south-facing wall is the only way to grow this plant in cool climates. During the first year after planting, tie shoots to bamboo canes that are attached at 45 degrees to horizontal wires fixed to the wall (see Apples and Pears, earlier in this chapter). Once established, in early summer of the second year after planting, pinch off the growing points of shoots when three leaves have been produced.

Any winter-damaged shoots or weak growth should be removed in late spring.

In warmer climates the fig can be grown as a free-standing tree. The only pruning necessary then is to thin out overcrowded branches and remove a portion of the old wood to encourage new, since figs produce their crop on one-year-old wood. The best time to prune is the dormant season to avoid excessive bleeding.

Fig trees are usually very vigorous and you may have to prune the roots to induce fruiting (see Chapter 1).

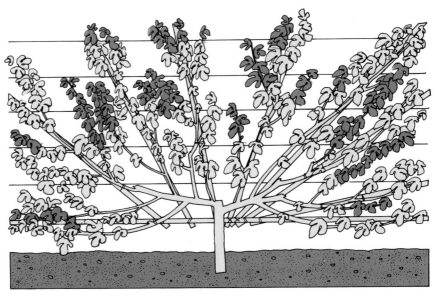

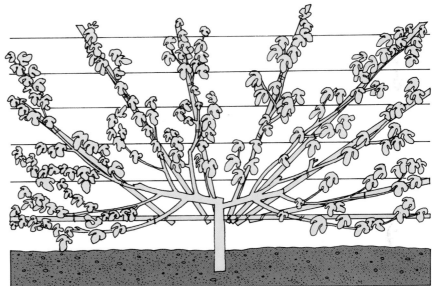

**ABOVE** Fan-train a fig as you do an apple or pear during the first year. In early summer the next year prune by pinching off the growing tips of all the shoots that have at least three leaves on them.

**LEFT** Corylus avellana, *showing male (long catkins) and female (small blossoms) flowers.*

**PRUNING FILBERT AND HAZEL TREES**

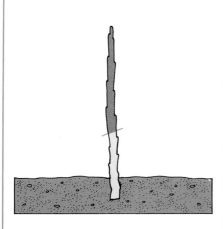

**1** After planting, cut the main stem back to three or four buds.

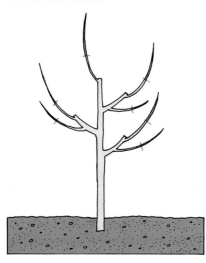

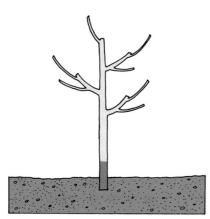

**2** In subsequent years, until the tree has reached a height of 6½ft (2m), prune new growth back to three buds, the uppermost facing upwards. Once the tree is established, do annual maintenance pruning.

76

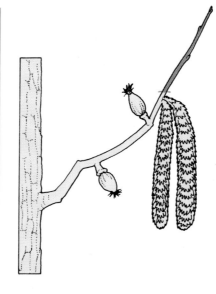

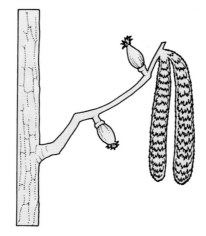

**3** Each spring, when the pollen is gone, prune fast-growing side shoots back to a catkin a few inches from the base of the shoot.

**PEACH AND NECTARINE BUSHES**
These are easily trained as free-standing trees.

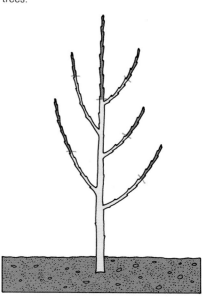

**1** Late in spring cut the one-year-old tree to 2ft (60cm) and remove the lateral tips that have died back over winter.

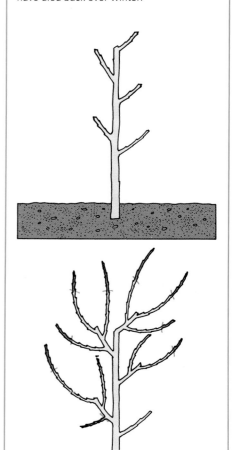

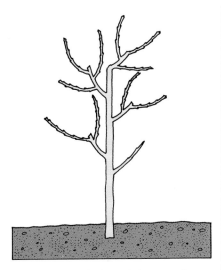

**2** Then thin out the lateral shoots so that there are only five or six strong and well-placed laterals left. In the following years prune in late spring to remove dead, diseased, and overcrowded wood.

**Mango** A warm climate is necessary for the plant to grow properly out of doors. Little pruning is necessary other than removing old spent and diseased wood. The tree is inclined to be over vigorous, and you may need to prune the roots.

**Mulberry** Train in the same way as for an open-center bush apple tree. Crossing branches should be removed to avoid rubbing. Prune weak and congested growth during the dormant season, since the plant is prone to bleeding at other times.

**Olive** When grown as a bush, pruning should be carried out as for *Olea* (see Chapter 3). Trees are pruned by removing old, congested wood and any suckers that arise from ground level.

**Papaya** This is another fruit tree for warm regions. Little pruning is necessary other than reducing the height if required; this is best done in spring.

**RIGHT** *Peaches and nectarines can be grown as free-standing trees or they can be fan-trained. They are susceptible to die-back and dead stems should be removed as soon as they are seen. These vigorous trees need constant attention during the active growing season so that they do not grow out of hand.*

**Peach and nectarine** Free-standing trees can be grown successfully in areas not subject to late frosts, which damage blossom. In late spring cut a one-year-old tree back to 2ft (60cm) and remove lateral tips that have died back. Thin out side shoots to leave five or six of the strongest and best-placed at regular intervals. In subsequent years, at the same time of year, remove overcrowded branches, diseased wood, and branches that have grown close to the ground.

In colder climates, nectarines are more likely to succeed against a south-facing wall or fence, pruned to a fan shape. (This is also a good solution for a gardener with limited space.) During the first spring after planting cut a one-year-old tree back to a lateral shoot or bud 2ft (60cm) from the ground. Retain two good lateral shoots or buds 10–12in (25–30cm) above the ground, one on either side of the main stem, and remove the rest.

The following summer, when the lateral shoots are 1½ft (45cm) long, tie them to canes fixed at an angle of 45 degrees to horizontal wires to create a Y-shaped plant. At the same time cut away the length of stem above the uppermost lateral. During late winter of the second year, cut each lateral back to a bud 1ft (30cm) from the main stem. In summer, when shoots have grown from the buds on the laterals, tie in the following to canes: ex-

tension growth at the shoot ends, two shoots growing on the upper side of each lateral, and one shoot on the lower side; remove all other buds and shoots.

During late winter of the third year, cut back each shoot to a bud 2ft (60cm) from the previous year's growth.

Once you have reached this stage, allow the tree to produce wood that will blossom and fruit for the first time. In late summer tie in the shoot that develops from the terminal bud on each branch, and also tie in other new shoots, provided they are spaced approximately 4in (10cm) apart; otherwise it is best to remove them. During the summer, pinch the tips of these shoots when they have grown to 1½ft (45cm) and tie them in. This growth will produce fruit the following year. Each year allow extension growth at the end of the stems to grow on until it has taken up the available space.

Once the main framework of the tree is established, yearly maintenance pruning is all that is needed. In spring remove new shoots growing toward or away from the wall, together with all but one growing from the base of fruit-bearing laterals produced the previous year (fruit is borne only on one-year-old wood); the shoot at the base of the lateral will replace it as fruit-bearing growth the following year. Fruit-bearing laterals produce sub-laterals; these are best pinched back to two leaves. Pinch subsequent shoots from the sub-laterals back to one leaf.

When you have gathered the fruit, remove any wood that has died back and cut back laterals that have borne fruit to replacement shoots. Tie these in.

**Pecan** This nut tree needs a warm climate to grow satisfactorily. Leave lateral shoots to grow into side branches for the first three years, until the young plant has become established; then during the dormant season in succeeding years gradually remove branches (two per year) from the base of the main stem until its lower 6½ft (2m) is bare.

**Plums** Due to their susceptibility to silver leaf disease, plum trees should be pruned either in summer after fruiting or in late spring so that the wounds heal quickly. Plums tend to be rather

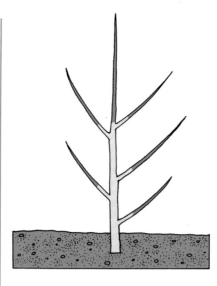

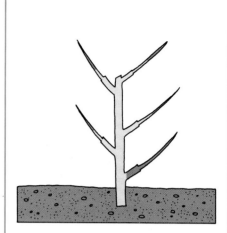

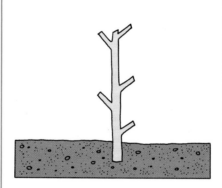

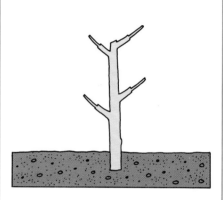

**PLUM TREES**
These are most often trained in the open-center bush form.
**1** In spring after planting, cut back one-year-old plants to 3ft (1m). Leave the laterals, even those low down on the stem, but cut them back hard.

**2** The following spring select four evenly spaced laterals and reduce them by half; then completely remove any other remaining shoots. The tree should now develop into its established shape, and all that will be necessary in future years is to prune out dead, diseased, and overcrowded wood.

vigorous; the easiest form to maintain is the bush. Cut back a one-year-old plant to 3ft (90cm) during the first spring after planting. The following spring select four uniform and evenly spaced laterals – ideally 3in (7.5cm) apart – and reduce their length by half. Remove remaining laterals completely. Once this framework is established, only maintenance pruning – removing any dead, crossing, or congested

branches – is necessary.

**Pomegranate** See *Punica* in Chapter 3.
**Quince** Little pruning is necessary, other than thinning out overcrowded branches and those that cross, together with straggling shoots. The best time to prune is during fall.

**Walnut** The only pruning needed is to remove dead or crossing branches. Do this in late spring or late summer so that wounds heal quickly.

CHAPTER NINE

# BERRIES AND FRUITING VINES

Unlike tree fruits, berries and vines do not require cross-pollination and so can be grown singly – an important point for gardeners for whom space is a problem. Gooseberries and red and white currants have the added advantage of being able to thrive against an east-facing wall, freeing other walls for more tender plants. Grown in a fan shape, they can also look very attractive.

**BELOW** *Blueberry bushes produce twiggy growth that should be pruned after fruiting.*

# POPULAR BERRIES AND VINES

**Blackberry and loganberry** These very vigorous plants need close control to prevent an unmanageable mass of growth developing. Before planting stretch horizontal wires between posts at 12in (30cm) intervals where the plant is to grow. After planting, cut the plants down to about 10in (25cm) above the ground. Tie the first year's canes (shoots) loosely to the wires on one side of the area allocated to the plant with string or raffia. Tie the following year's growth to the wires on the other side so that it is kept clear of the previous year's canes, which will bear the fruit. This prevents the two from becoming tangled, makes pruning easier and, if there is any disease on the older canes, prevents it from spreading to the new ones.

When fruiting is finished, cut the older, fruited canes out as soon as possible and as new replacement canes develop tie them in to the wires, spacing them evenly to make best use of the light and air available.

### TRAINING BLACKBERRIES AND LOGANBERRIES

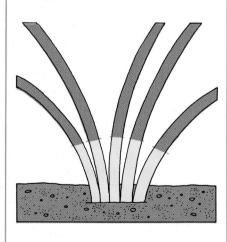

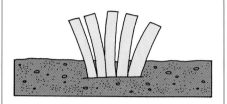

**1** After planting cut down the canes to within 10in (25cm) of the ground.

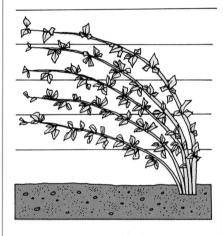

**2** When these canes grow, tie them to one side of the horizontal wires.

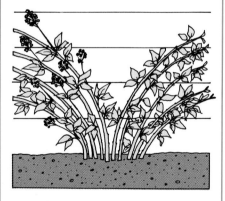

**3** During the following year tie the new growth to the other half of the horizontal wires, keeping it away from the previous year's canes.

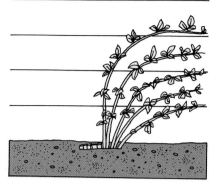

**4** Cut down the original canes once they have finished fruiting. Next year this growth should be tied up again and the other side's canes cut down after they fruit so that the growing and pruning cycle continues.

**ABOVE** *You can train loganberries in different ways, by tying the canes to horizontal wires stretched between posts. This is the "trombone" training method.*

**RIGHT** *During a blackcurrant bush's early years remove about one-quarter of the wood that has borne fruit immediately after the crop has been gathered; when the bush has matured, as here, up to one-third of the fruited wood may be cut out to ground level each year.*

**BELOW** *Loganberries, here, and similar plants are vigorous and need close supervision for best results.*

**ABOVE** *Prune blackcurrants hard, immediately after planting.*

**Blackcurrant** The best crop is obtained on wood made the previous year. Encourage vigorous growth by hard pruning: immediately after planting, cut back all shoots to 1in (2.5cm) above the ground. Remove any fruit buds that develop during the first year after planting so that the plant's resources are directed into producing as much growth as possible. In fall cut down to ground level any weak growth that has been produced during the year. The first crop will be forthcoming in the second year after planting. When the currants have been harvested, remove approximately a quarter of the fruited wood down to a bud close to the ground; in subsequent years this proportion can be increased to a third.

An alternative method is to cut down all the shoots after harvesting. This does mean, of course, that there will be no crop the following year, so to obtain fruit every year with this type of pruning two bushes that fruit on alternate years will be needed.

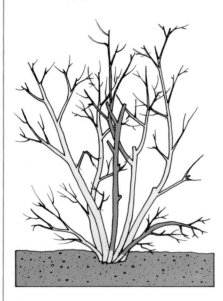

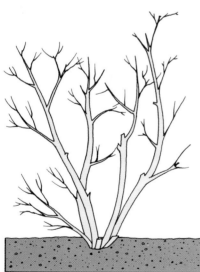

**ABOVE** Wait at least two years after planting to prune blueberries since pruning interferes with fruiting. Then each winter cut back a few of the older shoots to new growth or to ground level. Also cut out damaged and twiggy shoots.

**Blueberry** The blueberry seldom produces fruit in its early years. Since pruning delays fruiting, you should wait to make the first cut for at least two years after planting. Then cut back some of the older shoots to young growth or to ground level. Also cut off damaged and fruited twiggy shoots. This will encourage new growth and keep the bush tidy.

**Cranberry** This bush requires an acid soil subject to flooding during spring. Under those conditions, the plants require little attention to produce a good crop of berries. Pruning consists of cutting back the top growth close to the ground when it becomes congested. With the high-bush cranberry, trim plants if they become too tall and remove some old wood each year to prevent over-production of fruit, which may lead to biennial fruiting. If this does happen, it can be remedied by removing approximately one-third of the buds before they open in the fruiting year.

**Gooseberry** Gooseberry bushes are grown on a short "leg" (bare stem) to keep the fruit off the ground. To train a plant to this shape, choose three or four good shoots above the leg during the first winter after planting and cut them back by half. Some varieties produce shoots that droop, in which case cut back to an upward-facing bud. In the case of upright growers, cut back to

an outward-facing bud. Remove all other shoots, cutting flush with the stem. Follow the same procedure for the following two or three years. Cut lateral shoots back to 3in (7.5cm) and remove weak growth at the same time.

Large mature bushes will need thinning by removing old fruited wood. Keep the center of the bush open at all times. In midsummer encourage fruit bud development by reducing all laterals to five leaves. At the same time remove any shoot tips infected with mildew.

Gooseberries may also be pruned in a fan shape along a fence or wall: follow the instructions given for red and white currants.

**Grape** Early during the first winter after planting, cut back a young vine to three buds from the ground. The following winter select two of the subsequent shoots and cut each back to two buds. When growth begins during spring, remove all but one shoot on each of the previous year's shoots and as growth proceeds, tie the shoots loosely to a vertical post. Rub the other shoots out as soon as they appear.

The following winter cut back one of the shoots to mature wood (wood which has a brown, not a green, rind)

**BELOW** *Grow gooseberry bushes on a short leg so that the fruit does not spoil on the ground.*

**PRUNING GOOSEBERRIES**

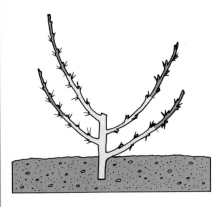

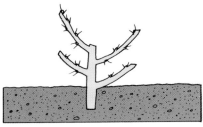

**1** Gooseberries are grown on a "short leg," (stem) with the 'bush' on top. The first winter after planting choose three or four strong shoots and cut them back by half; cut off any others. For the next two or three years cut these same shoots back by half again and remove all weak growth. Keep the "leg" free from side shoots.

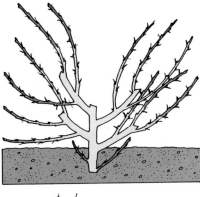

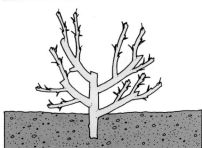

**2** Every winter after that thin out old, damaged, and unwanted growth.

**ABOVE** *Prune this year's growth back to three or four leaves in summer.*

and then tie it in to the lower horizontal wire. Cut the other shoot back to two buds. The retained shoot will produce fruiting laterals during the following summer, and you should pinch them out when the growing point reaches the top wire. Only one bunch of grapes should be allowed to develop on each fruiting lateral.

Tie the two new shoots on the other side of the plant on to the upright post to avoid wind damage.

During winter, cut the old spent rod that has produced the crop back to one bud; this will produce a shoot the following summer. Cut the existing new rod back to mature wood and tie it horizontally to produce fruit next summer. Repeat this alternate side-growing and cutting-back cycle.

**Raspberry** With summer-fruiting varieties, cut the canes during the winter

of planting down to 10in (25cm) from the ground. Tie in subsequent growth to horizontal wires stretched between posts. The first wire should be 3ft (1m) above the ground and the second should be 3ft (1m) above that so you have a support that is all together 6ft (2m) high. Fruit is produced on canes made the previous year. After gathering the fruit, cut the old canes out completely, right to the ground. In the meantime, new canes will have grown from ground level; choose about eight strong ones per plant and tie them in to fruit the following year. Remove the other, weaker canes. In spring either tip the top of the cane protruding above the highest wire or train it along the top wire. That fall and every fall thereafter cut down the fruit-bearing canes after harvest to maintain the annual cycle of new and mature canes.

Fall-fruiting raspberries produce fruit on current season's growth. After planting, cut down canes as for summer-fruit-

**TRAINING GRAPE VINES**

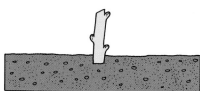

**1** Cut newly planted vines to within three buds of the ground during the first winter after planting.

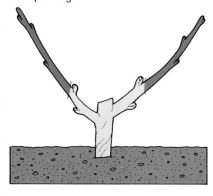

**2** The following winter select two of the shoots that develop and cut back to two buds. If any other shoots have grown, cut them off to the central vine.

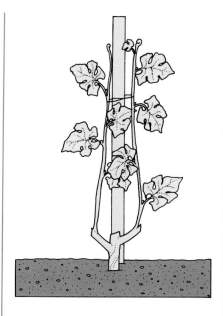

**3** In the spring cut off all but one shoot on each of the stems. As growth continues, loosely tie these shoots to a vertical post. Cut off any other shoots that develop.

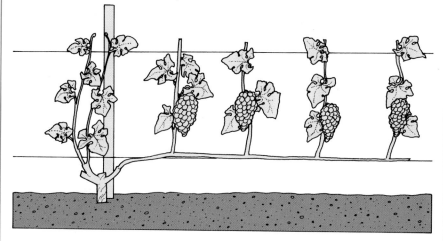

**5** During the following summer the shoot that was tied up will grow fruiting laterals; these should be pinched out when the growing point has reached the top wire.

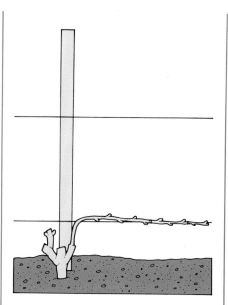

**4** The following winter cut back one of the shoots to mature wood and tie it to the lower horizontal wire. Cut back the other shoot to two buds.

**6** In the winter after cropping, cut back the old spent rod (here on the right) to one bud. Then cut back to mature wood the new rod grown last summer (here on the left) and tie it horizontally.

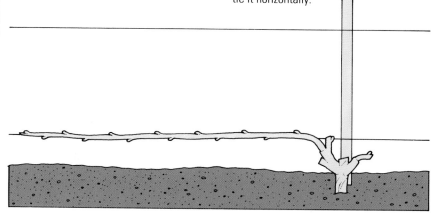

**TRAINING SUMMER-FRUITING RASPBERRIES**

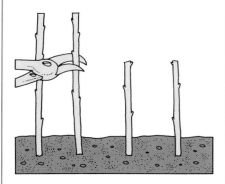

**1** The winter after planting, cut down all the canes to 10in (25cm) from the ground.

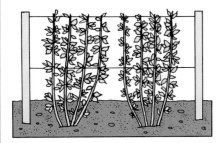

**2** As new canes grow, tie them to the horizontal wires. After these canes have fruited, cut them down to the ground, being careful not to cut down the new growth.

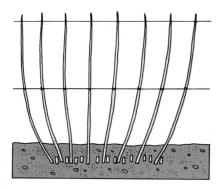

**3** Choose about eight of the strongest new canes per plant each year that have grown up from the ground and tie them to the wires. Cut out all the other new canes. These tied canes will fruit. During each spring either:

**4** cut off the tips of the canes growing above the top wire, or

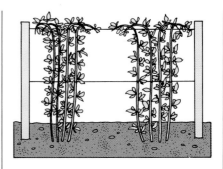

**5** train these canes along the top wire.

**BELOW** *Cut raspberry canes down to within 10in (25cm) of the ground after planting.*

ing varieties. Prune in late winter by cutting down all canes to just above soil level, leaving a few buds to grow and produce fruiting canes the following year. It is not necessary to tie the canes individually to wires; they can simply be allowed to interweave themselves between the wires.

**Red and white currants** These can be grown as bushes in the same way as gooseberries. (It should be noted that the growth habit of red and white currants is very different from that of blackcurrants.) Alternatively, they can be trained in a fan shape. To do this, cut the shoots down to two buds during the first winter after planting. Tie shoots that grow during the first summer to wire strained between vine eyes driven into a wall or fence. Tie shoots that develop the first summer to the wires, removing any that grow toward the wall or fence as soon as you notice them.

During the second winter, shorten each shoot by half to a side-facing bud. The following summer tie in the two top shoots arising from the shortened stems. In winter shorten these new shoots by half and the following summer tie in their top two shoots. Repeat this procedure each year until the allocated area has been covered. The framework stems should be approximately 6–10in (15–25cm) apart at their tips. Shorten lateral shoots to five leaves in summer, and remove very vigorous shoots completely. There is no need to prune moderately weak shoots.

Prune established plants in the summer in the same way, and again in winter by reducing laterals to three buds. Thin out congested and old fruited wood at the same time. Reduce suckers as soon as they arise from ground level by scraping back the soil and pulling them away.

**TOP LEFT** *In spring, cut off any summer-fruiting raspberry cane tips growing above the top wire.*

**LEFT** *All fall-fruiting raspberry canes are cut close to the ground in late winter.*

**TOP** Red currants remain healthy and productive when cordoned, as here.

**ABOVE** Red currants are also suitable for fan training.

# PRUNING CALENDAR

**I**f you have in your garden several shrubs and trees, some roses, a few fruit trees and vines, and a hedge or so, remembering what to prune when can be a formidable task indeed. Hopefully, this calendar will make the job a bit easier for you. Use it as a quick reference to seasonal pruning tasks, perhaps checking off in your mind as you glance through it at the start of each season what pruning might need to be done in your garden then.

These seasonal notes are intended as general guidelines only. Temperatures vary from region to region and indeed from year to year within a region. Such variations can influence the time of sap rise, flowering, and fruiting, which in many cases will then affect best pruning times.

Because this calendar includes only brief instructions on how to prune a particular plant, you will most likely want to refer to the body of the book for detailed pruning directions.

## EARLY SPRING

Extra-vigorous growth during the following season can often be encouraged by notching buds during the early spring: use a sharp knife to remove a small wedge of bark from just above the shoot bud to be stimulated. Notching is carried out on young trees within three years of planting. Nicking is the term used for removing a small wedge of bark from just below a growth bud to reduce the subsequent vigor of the resulting shoot.

## Shrubs

Remove spent shoots of *Abeliophyllum* by cutting back to the main stems once flowers have faded. Cut out winter-damaged and congested growth of the wood of *Acacia, Acer, Aesculus parviflora, Bouvardia, Chimonanthus; Choisya, Coronilla, Cotinus, Decaisnea, Elaeagnus, Eucryphia, Feijoa,* the deciduous kinds of *Euonymus, Fremontodendron, Hebe,* *Olea, Phlomis, Piptanthus* and *Punica.*

Remove weak growth and one-third of mature wood from *Alnus rugosa;* when extra vigor is needed, cut back remaining shoots. Cut stems of *Buddleia davidii* back to a bud within 18in (45cm) of the ground; very old plants are cut back to within two buds from the main framework. Prune *Caryopteris* by cutting back all stems to 6in (15cm) from the ground. *Ceratostigma* produces better flowers when the stems are cut back close to the ground at this time.

Cut frost-damaged shoots of *Elsholtzia* to ground level. Overgrown *Fatsia* should be pruned now. Cut off winter damage from *Hibiscus* and cut back previous season's growth to within three buds of the main framework. *Kerria* should have its winter damage pruned off and congested growth should be cut right to the soil level; also remove unwanted suckers. Keep *Ligustrum* bushy by pruning a few old stems right to the ground now and prune back the longer stems. Also prune *Lycium* every few springs to control its growth. When growing *Nyssa* as a shrub, control its growth by trimming now. Cut off old flowering shoots from *Olearia* and trim as needed to maintain shape. Give *Osmanthus* its first trimming of the year now.

Cut *Phygelius* shoots grown the previous year back to ground level. Remove completely one-third of the stems of *Physocarpus* and cut the remaining stems back to one-year-old wood. Cut out old spent stems of *Pontentilla.* Prune all growth of *Romnya* to within an inch or so of the ground. Cut down to the ground old stems of *Rubus* grown for their silver bark to encourage the growth of new silver stems. Hard pruning *Sorbaria* now will result in more flowers in summer.

*Spartium* may also be pruned lightly now for bigger flowers later, but be careful not to cut into mature wood because this plant does not easily pro-duce new growth. *Spiraea* plants grown for their foliage effect such as 'Gold Flame' are cut back hard; each stem is pruned to three or four buds from the ground level. This is the time to prune back by half last year's growth of *Thymus.* Cut out winter-damaged wood of *Vitex* and cut laterals back to the main framework.

## Vines and Climbers

*Ampelopsis* shoots that grew last year should be cut back to leave two or three buds. If not done in fall, congested growth of *Bougainvillea* should now be pruned back to the main framework and side shoots cut back to two or three leaves. Cut back winter-damaged *Callicarpa* to a healthy bud. On *Campsis* cut back the previous year's growth to two buds. Prune back winter-damage on *Carpenteria* and *Cestrum.* Remove half the length of *Celastrus* stems. Remove dead wood and crossing branches from *Chaenomeles;* shoots grown last year are cut back by one-third at the same time. Now is the time to prune back dead wood and shoot tips of summer- and fall-flowering species of *Clematis.*

Remove winter-damaged and invasive growth from *Hedera;* on variegated kinds look for and remove shoots that have reverted to all green. Cut out congested stems of *Lonicera;* when practical the growth should be removed from the support before pruning and then tied up again. Avoid touching the poisonous latex of *Periploca* when removing congested growth and weak shoots at this time. Very old *Polygonum* plants that are out of hand can be cut back hard to ground level; otherwise cut out damaged and dead stems, then reduce the length of shoots grown last year to two or three buds. Remove winter-damaged wood and invasive growth from *Pueraria* now; it can be pruned back hard if need be. Cut back *Solanum* to a strong lateral. Prune back last year's growth on *Tamarix gallica* and

*T. pentandra* by half now to prevent plants from getting too tall.

### Roses
Right after planting generally prune roses by cutting back dead stems to healthy wood just above a bud. Remove any weaker crossing stems and spindly stems to a bud. Stems of hybrid tea and floribunda roses are reduced in length to a bud 4–5in (10–12cm) from the ground immediately after planting. Very weak laterals are cut out completely and other side shoots should be cut back to leave 2in (5cm) of stem. After planting, climbing sports should be cut back to three to four buds from where the top growth arises from the rootstock.

Established bushes are pruned by first removing dead and diseased wood, then cutting out shoots growing toward the center leading to congestion; weak shoots are reduced to one or two buds. Some roses are strong growers, and the wood they made last year is cut back by half; on weak growers the stem length made last year is cut back by two-thirds.

### Hedges
*Fuchsia magellanica* grown as a hedge can be trimmed to shape now; the same treatment can be carried out on hedges of *Ribes sanguineum*.

### Ornamental Trees
Trim long shoots of deciduous and nonconiferous evergreen trees after planting. Those trees that are usually best pruned in early spring include: *Acer, Albizia, Arctostaphylos, Celtis* (now or in winter), *Cornus* (after flowers fade), *Euonymus, Fraxinus, Myoporum, Sparmannia, Taxus,* and *Umbellularia*.

Pinch side shoots of *Araucaria* to maintain shape. *Malus* can now be pruned by cutting congested spurs back to strong lateral shoots. Overgrown branches of *Abies* can be cut back to a bud or lateral shoot. Overgrown *Juniperus* is dealt with by cutting lateral shoots back to the main branches; avoid a "gappy" appearance since the plant will not regenerate from old wood. To control the growth of *Pinus* pinch new candles by half or completely pinch out some candles, being careful not to take out the entire candle cluster, which

will result in no new growth there. Pollard *Salix* now. This is also the time to start looking for and removing water sprouts from trees such as *Crataegus* and *Fraxinus*.

### Fruits and nuts
Prune new spring-planted fruit trees now. Prune cranberries now if necessary.

## LATE SPRING

### Shrubs
Reduce stems of *Abelia* to keep them within bounds; remove dead and winter-damaged stems back to a bud at the same time. Cut out the spent shoots of *Abeliophyllum* once the flowers have faded. *Abutilon* shoots damaged by frost should be cut hard back and cut other shoots back to a strong healthy lateral. When grown as a shrub, *Ailanthus* is cut back close to the ground at this time. Shoots of *Amorpha* damaged by frost should be cut back to healthy growth; old spent wood can be cut back to ground level to give space to new stems. Thin out sucker growth of *Aralia*.

Cut out spindly, straggly growth from *Arbutus*; an evergreen specimen can be cut back hard to bring it within bounds. Cut *Artemisia* hard back to encourage large leaves. Congested growth of *Arundinaria* is now cut back to ground level. Cut back the growth of *Atriplex* to within three buds from ground level. Cut away damaged shoots of *Azara*, together with any that spoil the desired shape and those that have flowered. Prune out dead wood of deciduous *Berberis* now or in early summer. Trim *Buxus* to shape and to remove winter damage.

Cut back untidy growth of *Calluna*; since this plant is reluctant to produce new shoots from old wood, cut last year's growth back by no more than half. Cut the stems of *Caryopteris* back to within 6in (15cm) of the ground. Remove winter damage and congested growth of *Cassia*. *Catalpa* grown as shrubs should be trimmed after flowering and winter damage removed. The summer-flowering evergreen *Ceanothus burkwoodii* and deciduous *Ceanothus* should be pruned by cutting the stems to within an inch or so of the ground. Do the

same for *Ceratostigma*. Thin out congested growth of *Clethra*. *Cornus* shrubs grown for their colored bark should now be cut back close to the ground. This is the time to trim and thin *Cotoneaster* and *Escallonia* if need be.

Reduce the stems of *Fuchsia* to ground level. After catkins have faded on *Garrya* cut off winter-damaged and congested growth. Prune congested and untidy growth of *Hamamelis* when flowers have faded. Trim *Hedysarum* as necessary. Prune the shoots of *Hydrangea paniculata* back close to the main framework. Thin out *H. macrophylla* by pruning old wood and remove spent flower heads. Cut *Hypericum* shoots back by half. Prune winter-damaged and congested growth from *Indigofera*. Remove dense growth from *Jasminum nudiflorum* after flowering and prune back *J. humile* if needed.

Cut back about half the stems of *Leucothoe* after flowering; plants out of control can be cut back to soil level at the expense of the current year's flowers. Remove old *Leycesteria* stems, retaining those with bright rind. Cut back the previous year's growth of *Lippia* to within a few buds of the main framework. Shape *Mahonia* by cutting it back after the flowers drop. Prune only part of the plant each year to ensure berry production. Lightly cut back *Melaleuca*. Prune back congested growth of *Myrica*. Cut back the shoots of *Perovskia* to within a couple of inches of the woody base. Prune back *Osmaronia* right after flowering. Cut back leading shoots of *Ribes* by half after flowering; old wood should be thinned out at the same time. Silver-barked *Rubus* is pruned by removing old canes. *Salix* grown for its colored stems should now be cut back to within about 3in (7.5cm) of the ground. For *Salix* that are grown primarily for their catkins, thin out congested growth once the catkins have faded. *Sambucus* can now be cut back to last year's growth to encourage larger flowers and more foliage. Cut back straggly shoots of *Santolina* and *Senecio*. Dead-head *Syringa* flowers once they had faded. Remove old spent wood from *Zenobia*.

### Vines and climbers

Remove dead wood from *Actinidia*. Cut back close to the ground *Humulus* if it is unruly; otherwise thin out congested growth. Remove outward-growing shoots and spent flower stems of *Hydrangea petiolaris*. Trim *Itea* now. Cut away a portion of the old stems of *Kadsura* to promote growth for enhanced fall tints. Vigorous growth of *Solanum crispum* can be pruned back to within 6in (15cm) of the main framework at this time. Cut out winter damage now on *Tibouchina* as growth buds become active; prune back spent wood and weak growth to the main framework.

### LATE SUMMER

#### Shrubs

After summer flowering, a number of shrubs can be pruned back to new lateral shoots to keep them trim and well shaped. These include *Bignonia, Buddleia globosa, B. alternifolia, Caragana, Dipelta, Kolkwitzia,* deciduous *Magnolia, Myrtle, Raphiolepis, Piptanthus, Ulex,* and *Weigelia*.

Lightly trim *Embothrium* after flowering if it needs shaping. Cut out weak shoots of *Exochorda* and at least half of those that have flowered. Lightly cut back stems of *Genista* once flowers have faded; avoid cutting into old wood. Give *Osmanthus* its second trimming now or in fall. *Rosmarinus* shoots are cut back by half after flowering, and the previous year's growth can be pruned back to half to promote bushy growth. *Wisteria* grown as a shrub should be pruned after flowering by cutting stems back by half.

### Vines and climbers

Remove shoots of *Akebia* that have flowered, then thin out congested growth. Reduce long shoots of *Aristolochia* by half and cut out congested growth after flowering.

Spring- and early-flowering *Clematis* are now pruned by cutting out old spent wood. Remove faded flower clusters from *Clianthus*. Cut back old *Desfontainea* wood to strong lateral shoots. Vigorous *Pyracantha* shrubs are pruned by pinching back new growth to four or five leaves. To control growth of *Vitis*

*coignetiae* cut back new shoots to within bounds.

### Hedges

Trim the hedges *Crataegus monogyna, Elaeagnus pungens, Fagus sylvatica, Griselinia, Hippophae rhamnoides, Ilex aquifolium,* and *Philadelphus* now. *Euonymus* and *Ligustrum* hedges may also be trimmed again now if needed. After flowering, trim the hedges *Escallonia macrantha, Lavandula spica, Santolina chamaecyparissus,* and *Weigela florida*.

### Ornamental trees

Rejuvenate weak *Chamaecyparis* trees by cutting back current season's growth by one-third. *Cedrus* can be pruned by lightly cutting back the current growth to a bud or side shoot; thin if needed. To control the growth of *Juniperus* current season's growth may be cut back now by half. *Liriodendron* can be pruned now, but do so minimally because its wounds are slow to heal. *Salix* may be pruned now or in fall.

### Fruits and nuts

Summer prune fruit trees to reduce vigor and encourage fruit bud development. Prune plum trees after fruiting if it was not done in spring. Prune filbert and hazel nut trees by snapping off the vigorous side shoots 6in (15cm) from the base to encourage spurs to develop. Prune walnuts now if not done in spring.

Cut out completely canes from summer-fruiting raspberries, loganberries, and blackberries after fruiting.

### EARLY FALL

#### Shrubs

Straggly *Calycanthus* shoots should be cut back after flowering and old unproductive wood can be removed at the same time. Cut out spent stems of *Decaisnea* after flowers fade. Reduce the length of *Lavandula* stems by one-half after flowers fade. Give *Osmanthus* its second trimming now if not done in summer. Continue to prune shoots of *Philadelphus* back to a strong lateral once flowers have faded. Cut out untidy *Phlomis* growth and pinch back regrowth from summer.

### Hedges

The hedge *Syringa microphylla* can be trimmed after flowering.

### Ornamental trees

Trim long shoots of deciduous and nonconiferous evergreen trees after planting. Prune the evergreen *Magnolia* and *Salix*, if it was not done in summer and is needed.

### Fruit and nuts

Prune blackcurrants.

### LATE FALL

#### Shrubs

Prune back shrubs liable to be damged by strong wind. After flowering, remove those shoots of *Callistemon* that have flowered; be careful not to hard prune because growth is minimal from dormant buds. This is the time to prune evergreen *Magnolia* and tie new growth to supports. Cut old *Nerium* wood back to main framework and faded flowering shoots to previous year's growth. Cut back invasive shoots of *Rubus*, other than those grown for silver stems which should be pruned in spring.

### Vines and climbers

Cut back congested growth of *Bougainvillea* to main framework by cutting side shoots to two or three leaves. Prune fall-flowering *Camellias* after flowers have faded.

### Roses

Cut back old flowered shoots of climbing roses to within 3in (7.5cm) of the main stem. Cut back rambler rose stems to a strong lateral, thin out vigorous growers by removing very old stems to ground level; flowered laterals are cut back to within 3in (7.5cm) from the main stem. On hybrid tea and floribunda roses cut out invasive growth to strong laterals; anything more severe can ruin the shape of the plants.

### Hedges

The fast-growing hedges of *Ligustrum* and *Lonicera nitida* can be trimmed again now if needed.

### Ornamental trees

*Betula* may be pruned now or in early winter. *Cercidiphyllum* may be thinned, and *Nyssa* can be pruned after its colorful leaves have fallen. *Populus* and *Ulmus* can also be pruned at this time.

### Fruit and nuts

Prune quince now.

## EARLY WINTER

Over-vigorous plants can be checked by root pruning during the winter. Root prune young plants by pushing the sharp blade of a spade into the soil at a distance equal to half the height of the plant – in a circle all around the plant. For a large tree or shrub dig a trench halfway around the plant 2–4ft (60cm–1.2m) away from the trunk and cut through any roots thicker than 1in (2.5cm), keeping damage to thinner roots to a minimum. Also cut downward-growing taproots. It is prudent to treat only half the root system (a 180-degree area) one year and the other half the following year, so that the plant will not suffer too much while you are checking its growth.

### Shrubs

Cut back the stems of *Buddleia davidii* halfway to avoid wind rock during strong winds. Prune back shoots of *Colutea* close to the main stems; also thin congested growth.

Rejuvenate old *Syringa* plants now by cutting out congested growth and shortening branches by one-third. *Vitis coignetiae* can be thinned out now. Prune *Wisteria* now by cutting stems shortened in summer to two or three buds and cut out congested growth.

### Roses

On climbing sports prune back the shoot tips to strong growth and tie to supports. Cut back old shoots that have flowered to two buds and remove congested growth.

### Ornamental trees

If needed and not done in fall, prune *Betula*. Prune *Celtis* now or wait until spring. This is the time to prune *Amelanchier*, *Ailanthus* (look for water sprouts too), *Carpinus*, *Castanea* (look for water sprouts), *Crataegus*, *Morus*, and *Ostrya*. *Davidia* can be pruned now but do so minimally since its wounds are slow to heal. *Rhus* may be pruned but it is important to wear gloves so as not to be irritated by its sap. On weeping trees that have not reached their desired height cut the leader and lateral shoots back to two or three buds each year at this time.

## LATE WINTER

### Shrubs

Cut out weak growth in *Alnus rugosa* plus about one-third of the mature wood when catkins have fallen. Remove old woody suckers from *Amelanchier*. Invasive *Aronia* suckers can now be removed together with congested growth. Congested growth of *Chaenomeles* should be cut out. *Ilex* can be cut back to a bud or lateral, but avoid cutting into old wood. Cut back stems of *Lespedeza* to ground level, unless growing in a warm climate when congested growth is cut back to the main framework.

### Hedges

Trim *Berberis thunbergii* now.

### Ornamental trees

*Abies* may be pruned now or you can wait until spring. Remove congested growth from *Aesculus* and *Crataegus* as well, crossing branches of *Mespilus* and those that touch the ground.

### Fruits and nuts

For apples and pears in their first four year's of growth prune back hard by cutting the previous season's growth back to within 3in (7.5cm) of their base. For more established apples and pear varieties that bear fruit on their spurs, lightly cut extension shoots on the end of the leaders. Healthy mature apple and pears should be pruned annually now by shortening the extension shoots and cutting back the laterals fairly close to their bases. Old overgrown apple and pear trees should be cut back to the main branches.

Thin out congested growth and crossing branches of fig, pecan, and mulberry trees. Winter prune fanned peaches and nectarines.

Prune new fall and winter-planted fruit bushes and canes. Prune blueberries and grape vines. Winter prune red and white currants. Cut back fall-fruiting raspberries.

# GLOSSARY OF TERMS

**apex** The top of a plant.

**apical bud** A bud at the end of a stem.

**bark ringing** The removal of a narrow ring of bark from the tree trunk.

**biennial bearing** When a plant produces a very heavy crop one year and little or none the next.

**branch bark ridge** A ridge that can be seen at the junction of the branch and the trunk of most trees.

**bush** A low, dense shrub or fruit plant.

**callus** Plant cells produced by the plant to heal a wound.

**candle** Extension growth of pine branches.

**central leader** The main stem.

**conifer** Mainly cone-bearing plants, usually evergreen.

**cordon** A plant trained as a single stem. (There are also double and triple cordons.)

**crotch** The angle between two branches.

**crown** The arrangement of branches at the top of a stem.

**dead-heading** The removal of faded flower heads.

**deciduous** A woody plant that sheds its leaves naturally during fall.

**dehorning** Severe shortening of a branch.

**disbudding** The removal of unwanted flower buds from around the main bud.

**dormancy** The resting period of a plant.

**evergreen** A plant that bears foliage throughout the year.

**extension growth** New growth arising from the previous season's shoots.

**fan** A plant trained so that the branches radiate fan-wise from the main stem.

**firm wood** Branches and shoots with tough rind.

**floribunda** Roses also known as cluster-flowered bush roses; the flowers come in trusses, clusters, or many stems.

**flush cut** A cut that is made close and flush with another part of the plant.

**framework** The main branch skeleton of a plant.

**gummosis** An exudation of a gumlike substance from cherry and plum trees.

**half-standard** A tree or shrub with a clear stem or trunk that is three to four feet tall, which is shorter than that of a standard.

**head** The uppermost part of a plant, the branches above the trunk, or stem. Also known as the crown.

**hybrid tea** Roses also known as large-flowered bush roses. A rose with shapely buds which develop into large or medium-sized flowers.

**lateral** A shoot growing from a main stem.

**leader** The main stem of a plant.

**maiden** A young tree with only one-year-old growth above ground.

**mature wood** Growth that has completed its extension longitudinally.

**new wood** Growth made during the current season.

**nicking** Cutting into the rind below a bud.

**notching** The removal of a small wedge of bark above a bud.

**old wood** Growth made before the current season.

**on year** The year when fruit is produced by a plant subject to biennial bearing.

**open center** A plant trained so that the center of the head is devoid of branches.

**pinch** To remove a portion of stem with finger and thumb.

**pollarding** Cutting tree branches back hard. It is often carried out on plants with colorful bark such as *Salix* (willow).

**pruning** The removal of any part of the plant by cutting or pinching.

**pyramid** A plant with branches growing over the length of the main stem, with the lower branches longer than those above.

**renewal pruning** A method of pruning which encourages new growth to replace that which has borne fruit.

**reversion** A shoot with totally green leaves growing from a plant that normally has other than green leaves. Also a disease of blackcurrants.

**root stock** The underground part of a plant that gives rise to the shoot.

**soft wood** Young stems devoid of tough stems or bark.

**side shoots** See laterals.

**spur** A short, jointed twig containing fruit buds.

**spur system** A collection of spurs on a branch.

**standard** A tree or shrub with a clear stem or trunk that is almost five to six feet tall. (See half-standard.)

**stopping** The removal of the growing point of a plant.

**stub** A portion of stem or branch that has been left after pruning.

**sub-lateral** A shoot growing from a lateral.

**sucker** A shoot growing from ground level or below; also a name sometimes given to water sprouts.

**tap root** The main root of a plant.

**tie down** A method of training roses so that the stems are trained close to the ground on horizontal wires, or by being pegged down.

**tie in** To tie to a support.

**tip bearer** A plant that produces fruit buds at the end of shoots.

**truss** A compound stalk with flowers or fruit.

**union** The junction between shoot and root.

**water sprout** Vigorous and sappy growths often arising from around pruning cuts.

# INDEX